INTERCESSION,
Thrilling and Fulfilling

JOY DAWSON

YWAM
PUBLISHING
A Ministry Of Youth With A Mission
P.O. Box 55787, Seattle, WA 98155

YWAM Publishing is the publishing ministry of Youth With A Mission. Youth With A Mission (YWAM) is an international missionary organization of Christians from many denominations dedicated to presenting Jesus Christ to this generation. To this end, YWAM has focused its efforts in three main areas: 1) Training and equipping believers for their part in fulfilling the Great Commission (Matthew 28:19). 2) Personal evangelism. 3) Mercy ministry (medical and relief work).
For a free catalog of books and materials write or call:
YWAM Publishing
P.O. Box 55787, Seattle, WA 98155
(425) 771-1153 or (800) 922-2143
e-mail address: 75701.2772 @ compuserve.com

Intercession, Thrilling and Fulfilling

ISBN 1-57658-006-7

Printed in the United States of America.

Dedication

I am deeply grateful to my dear, committed intercessor friends for the significant role they play. Without them, the effectiveness of my ministry would be substantially lessened. They are among my most treasured gifts from God. It is a joy to honor them and dedicate this book to them. Their prayers helped to birth it.

Acknowledgments

As at all times, and especially while writing this book, I was vividly aware of my desperate need of the inspiration, direction, and energizing of the Holy Spirit. I also never felt so dependent on the prayers of others during a writing project as I did while working on this one.

I am greatly indebted to my precious husband Jim, without whose willing and able help in numerous areas, this project would not have been accomplished.

My sincerest thanks to my excellent, former secretary Kay Matta for her invaluable assistance in typing the manuscript. I also appreciate the editorial suggestions given me by my dear friend Len LeSourd before his death. And I'm very grateful for the staff at YWAM Publishing who have been wonderfully cooperative. My special thanks to Jim Drake, the editor, who was a delight to work with.

Note to the Reader

Any reader in the United States or Canada who feels the need to find someone to partner with in prayer for serious, personal needs can contact an organization called Breakthrough,[1] which has 3,500 intercessors whose sole function is to pray for the personal needs of people who seek help. Each prayer request goes out to five intercessors for a period of twenty-one days for prayer. This wonderful ministry is supported solely by the freewill offerings of God's people.

There are also Christian television and radio networks, plus churches with telephone counseling ministries, that hurting people are encouraged to call for help. The reader will understand that the author is unable to personally meet such needs.

---

1. Breakthrough, P.O. Box 121, Lincoln, Virginia 22078-0121 U.S.A.

Foreword

*"He makes my feet like the feet of deer, and sets
me on my high places. He teaches my hands to make
war, so that my arms can bend a bow of bronze."*
—Psalms 18:33-34

I saw a hot air balloon take off yesterday, and something in me leaped upward again.

Whenever I see the surreal sight of one of those magnificently colored, medieval-like objects becoming airborne, whether against the backdrop of a radiant dawn, or hanging like a tree-ornament on the face of a verdant hillside, I'm transfixed—caught with a sense of timelessness.

I am drawn to that scene just now, because in inviting you to plunge into the wealth and beauty contained in this book, that imagery seems to provide striking parallels.

First, you are on the brink of a magnificent and mighty, *uplifting* experience. Just as the balloon rises with the heat surging into its billowing frame, there is a buoyancy awaiting you. And believe me, this isn't "hot air." Rather, these pages provide a fire-filled atmosphere, warmed by the presence of the Holy Spirit! I believe that as you read—just as with balloon travel—you'll find yourself lifted to a broader perspective and enlarged with a new vision.

Second, you're also about to be brought to new boundaries of possibility, because *elevation* isn't all a balloon gains—the winds surrounding it bring *transportation,* too. There is movement that unveils ever-increasing and expanding horizons. That's exactly what I have witnessed taking place in recent years regarding the precious and powerful truths of *intercessory prayer.*

As winds of spiritual renewal continually spread, the Church our Jesus has birthed in this generation is being borne upward and forward by a sweeping spirit of prayer. The balloon, so to speak, has been advancing with the Spirit's gentle power (the wind) just as it has been ignited by His mighty presence (the fire). Get ready for both! You're about to tap into rich resources that will waft you higher; that will deepen your grasp of those prayer-secrets that have made God's people powerful throughout earlier eras. Here are timeless truths, but brought alive today with new splendor and power suited to today's challenges and opportunities.

Finally, the balloon is beautiful—brilliant in its color, creative in its design—and so is this book! This isn't surprising at all, considering the loveliness and steadfastness of God's grace which has been displayed through the life and ministry of the writer.

Joy Dawson is a teacher who makes both the beauty and the truth of God's word *live* with color and creativity. However, as quick as this dear woman's mind is, the brilliance in her writing is more than the product of human intellect alone. You are stepping into the pages of a book that is born of long travail as well as the fruitful experience of years.

For years now, I have been privileged to be called "Pastor" by Joy and Jim Dawson. Most recently, all their friends—and certainly, a host within our congregation—have been touched by the grace, patience and faith that they have both shown during the season of physical trial Joy has endured. If loving prayers could provide an instant answer, her pain would have been absent long ago. But this has not been a short battle.

It may seem paradoxical to some, that a book on prayer's power and the truth of the promise that "all things are possible to him who believes," would be written by a person living through the pain and struggle of a not-yet-completely-answered prayer. However, in truth, that fact only increases the credibility of the writer's grasp of the subject matter here, because Joy and Jim illustrate *that consummate, biblical faith in God's absolute faithfulness* which, ultimately, is the only real certainty that any of us have when we pray.

So, it is my pleasure to introduce you to a book which deserves to be a text for every Bible student and a tool in the hands of every Christian—a means for us all to leverage our spiritual insight and power to new heights. Now, please, take it in hand—and prepare for a mighty "sky-ride." I predict a new "high" for you, and best of all this is the kind from which you never have a post-trip let down!

As the horizons of intercessory possibilities expand before you, you will first be captivated by the vision. But as you continue, I assure you—you'll become imprinted with the grandeur of this truth: *It's the people who "ride the high places" with God who, in partnership with Him, determine the affairs of humankind living in the valleys and plains below!*

Jack W. Hayford, Senior pastor
The Church On The Way

Van Nuys, California
May 1997

Table of Contents

Preface

The purpose for writing this book is to inspire, encourage, and motivate readers to put into personal practice the biblical principles contained within this book's pages. I have tried to balance inspirational writing with simple, biblical instruction. Many of the chapters are how-to oriented; designed so that each chapter can stand alone and be used as a guide for an exhilarating, fulfilling time of intercession in each area. Consequently, a certain amount of overlapping has been necessary.

I trust you'll be forever ruined for the ordinary as you discover or rediscover the wonders of cooperating with God in shaping the course of history through intercession. It happened to me. It can happen to you.

I'm so thankful that we have a record of some of the prayers of Jesus, along with those of the Old and New Testament prophets, and the apostle Paul. And aren't we glad that we got to listen in on David's prayer of repentance and Hannah's cry for spiritual ambition and fulfillment? What a wealth of learning we would have missed had we never heard their heart cries to God.

I am aware of Jesus' words of admonition in Matthew 6:6 to go into our rooms and pray to God in secret. A reward is subsequently promised. Obviously God in His wisdom uses this as a test of our motives. We will all be tested at varying times regarding our response to His words. However, I find in the Bible both in Jesus' life on earth and in the lives of others that this is not an absolute. Otherwise, we would never know when, where, or what these people prayed.

Ecclesiastes 3:7b says there is *"a time to be silent and a time to speak."* For many years I've said that unless the Holy Spirit clearly prompts us to do so, it is wiser not to share what God reveals to us in intercession. I still believe that. However, the thing that impresses God the most is obedience. When He tells us that it's time to share for the benefit of others, our love for Him will be measured by our obedience to His clear directions. For this reason, I have included a number of personal experiences with intercessory prayer in this book. I am acutely aware that anything God has done in and through me is strictly the outworking of His amazing grace and unending mercy.

My favorite verse is *"For from him and through him and to him are all things. To him be the glory forever! Amen"* (Romans 11:36).

1

Adventure and
Friendship with God

*I*t was so cold outside that an orange froze almost as soon as it was peeled. The small team of young people from Youth With A Mission (YWAM),[1] representing several nations, had mixed feelings as they approached the university campus. This was definitely "Mission Unknown" in a country where the government forcefully forbids all Christian activity.

Would the young people have any opportunity to witness about their faith in the Lord Jesus? Would they be arrested and possibly imprisoned? If they were, who would ever know? Since it was a few days before Christmas, these young missionaries would no doubt have private thoughts about the stark contrast to Christmas back home. Underlying their feelings of foreboding was a deep, unexplainable sense of anticipative adventure that they'd never before known. After all, there was only one explanation for their being here...GOD. They were experiencing the greatest adventure known to man...following Him.

---

1. Youth With A Mission is a multidenominational, international Christian organization with a threefold emphasis: evangelism, training and mercy ministries. Founded in 1960, YWAM currently has over five hundred fifty operating locations in one hundred thirty countries.

Only about a week before, the team members had been put together in a prayer group at a missionary training center in a large cosmopolitan city where they had been in training. Their assignment was to seek God as to the nation or nations for which God wanted them to pray that day. As the team members followed the directions of the Holy Spirit, first a nation, and then one particular city in that nation, was impressed upon their spirits. These seekers of God were experiencing the thrill of "walking on the water" in the exciting ministry of intercession.

God's burden for that particular city was being shared with the young people as they continued to pray fervently for God to move in mighty ways to extend His Kingdom, so much so, that at the end of the assigned hour, each one had a compelling desire to go to that city as soon as possible. This surprised them as much as it did the leaders to whom they had submitted their impressions.

Finally, after much prayer, God confirmed that He was sending the team out to be part of the answer to their recent prayers. They watched God work a series of divine interventions related to hurriedly obtained visas and financial releases. The group departed greatly encouraged. God had directed them to pray for the nation they now found themselves in. A little later, God directed one of the leaders of the training center to join, encourage, and take the mail to the team.

For the first three days, the only direction from the Lord was to intercede for the city, which the group did diligently. At times they took intercession walks around the city. On one such occasion, one of the girls met an English language teacher from the local teachers training college. The woman was thrilled to meet a native English speaker, and invited the team members to visit her two classes, comprising teachers from around the nation who had come specially to improve their English.

The woman asked whether the team could possibly explain to the teachers the meaning of Christmas. There were thirty people in each class whose ages ranged from 19 years to mid-50s. The missionaries, who understood that this was an incredible opportunity beyond anything they could have imagined, were delighted to oblige!

The group presented a drama of the Christmas story to these people, who knew little or nothing of the gospel. Jeff, the group leader, narrated through an interpreter. The young people taught the teachers Christmas carols by the same method. Their audiences were enthralled as Jeff explained that Christmas was a time of celebration of God's gift to the world of His Son, the Lord Jesus Christ. They were deeply moved as they heard about the suffering of Jesus on the cross for their sins. Some repeated the words responsively, and some wept openly. Their hearts had been wonderfully prepared by the Holy Spirit as a result of all the advance intercession. Consequently, many expressed a great desire to receive God's gift of salvation.

Aware of this, Jeff turned to the person in charge of each class and offered to help the class receive God's gift, despite the fact that for many years large numbers of Christians had been severely persecuted in this country. Each official gave Jeff the go ahead.

Jeff then knelt in the middle of the classroom and led the group in a responsive prayer involving a total commitment of their lives to the Lord Jesus Christ. Immediately, everyone was overwhelmed by the presence of the Lord and manifest great joy. Jeff wisely lost no time in teaching the group how to hear God's voice, and the importance of obedience to God's direction.

The next day the mission team returned with Bibles in the people's language. The team members were given permission to distribute the Bibles and teach from them in both classes for another two hours. They continued to meet with the teachers for several days.

Soon after, Jeff told me this remarkable story when I was speaking at a conference in the city where the YWAM team had held that first significant prayer meeting. Jeff was still noticeably overcome and awed by the wonder of what God had privileged him to be a part of—not the least being the revelation that God had given him on the spot of how to explain the gospel to people who had never heard it, and who were from a completely different culture.

Later, one of the team members shared more of the story with me. On one occasion, when the team did a worship dance to the Lord arranged to the music of "Sing Hosanna," the teachers were greatly impressed and begged the missionaries to teach the dance to them. They taught three of the women the dance movements. A few days later, the mission team members were invited to a Christmas party. To their amazement, the whole class performed the worship dance without a mistake. Truly amazing in a country overtly hostile to Christianity!

While in the same city, one of the team members befriended a teenage girl who had been praying for two years for a Bible. When her prayers had been answered, the girl readily listened to the gospel story and genuinely committed her life to the Lord Jesus Christ. Other foreign Christians in that city discipled the girl after the team had left. Eventually the Lord called the girl to take the gospel to one of the unreached people groups in her home province. To prepare herself, the girl went to the university to study that people group's language.

Who knows how many ripples of divine purpose are still flowing from God's direction to a handful of young people who made intercession for the nations a priority.

You may be thinking, "Wow, what a story! I wish I could hear God's voice and pray like that!" You can. Those young people in that discipleship training school were simply following the steps from my teaching on "Principles for Effective Intercession" (outlined in chapter 7). When applied, the steps never fail to produce an interesting, significant, and deeply fulfilling time of prayer. There's never a dull or wasted moment. It will take more time in preparation before you launch out in prayer than when you pray "off the top of your head," but I can promise you that the rewards far outweigh the small price.

If you have ever attended a dull prayer meeting, God wasn't given the opportunity to be in charge. There's nothing dull about fulfilling God's conditions to hear His voice when you think about who God is! He is the most exciting Being in the universe. I never lose the wonder of the fact that He longs to communicate with us and intends for communication to be a normal part of our relationship with Him. God frequently speaks to His children who believe and expect that He will. What joy! What fulfillment! How fabulous He is!

Why is intercession such a wonderful way of experiencing God? Because intercession is praying as directed and energized by the Holy Spirit for others. In doing so, we become recipients of part of God's mind and heart for them. God thinks the most merciful, loving, tolerant thoughts, filled with spiritual ambition for everyone, which means that He shares part of Himself with us. Nothing can change us more quickly to become like Him. We could all do with plenty of that.

In my life, the greatest times of dynamic spiritual action, revelation, and the sense of God's presence and power have been during times of worship and prayer. That's when I've experienced

- the deepest moves of God's Spirit to change me.
- the greatest revelation of my own heart.
- the greatest revelation of the heart of God.
- the greatest spiritual unity with others.
- the deepest moves of God's Spirit through me on behalf of others.
- the greatest spiritual authority.
- the greatest victories over the powers of darkness.
- the greatest releases of faith.
- the moments of greatest intimacy of friendship with God.

Worship and prayer dull? Hardly! They lead to adventure and friendship with God.

2

Revelation in Intercession

God links earnest prayer with divine revelation in Jeremiah 33:3, *"Call to me and I will answer you and tell you great and unsearchable things you do not know."* The following account vividly illustrates this truth.

In May 1973 I was speaking at a church in California during its missions convention. While there, I had the privilege of meeting one of God's choice disciples, Arnie Abrahamson. At the time, Arnie was a Wycliffe missionary from the jungles of Brazil on furlough in the United States. I listened to the gripping story of this man's burden for three unreached tribes and his many lone attempts to reach them with the gospel. Arnie shared about the numerous times he'd faced death through lack of food, illness, and murder attempts by the natives. Two things became vividly clear to me:

1. I was to become an intercessor for this man and his vision.
2. I was to encourage others to do the same.

The following week I was teaching in Switzerland at a YWAM school of evangelism. I told Paul Hawkins, one of the leaders, that I had brought with me a tape of Arnie's story, and I shared with him some of the facts. Paul didn't try to hide his excitement and amazement, as he in turn recounted what had taken place in his intercession-for-the-nations group the week before. As the young people had diligently applied the ten principles for effective intercession, God, as usual had given them remarkable revelation.

To one was given the impression of the nation of Brazil. Another was impressed to intercede for a missionary working alone in the jungles of Brazil. Another said, "I believe God is showing me that the man is working with the Wycliffe Bible translators." For some time the Holy Spirit burdened this group with the needs of a man who they didn't know existed, and for the souls of the tribes the missionary was seeking to reach with the gospel.

The next morning, another staff member, who had not been able to attend the intercession group the previous morning and had heard nothing of what was prayed for, led the group in prayer. God did it again—He gave the woman detailed revelation of Arnie and his needs without any prior knowledge on her part of who he was. This was an undeniable confirmation that the group had been hearing from God. Imagine the encouragement when they heard Arnie's story on my tape verifying everything in detail!

The greatest encouragement was kept for Arnie himself. I returned to California and told him how God had uniquely singled him out and made him the focus of intercession through a group of young people on the other side of the world who had taken time to pray for the nations.

You may be thinking how relatively easy it would be for these young people to hear God compared to yourself in your circumstances. They were surrounded by teachers who were inspiring them, and they had the advantage of the group dynamics that motivates faith. I can understand that reaction. It's a legitimate one. But let me encourage you by saying that hearing God's voice, whether in intercession or at other times, is for every child of God (John 10:27).

Every Believer has the privilege of being used by God in effective intercession. *Not* just the favored few. *Not* just little old ladies who are not able to do much else. *Not* just people who are "specially called to the ministry of intercession," as I so often hear. Intercession is *everyone's* ministry, just as worshiping and witnessing are. And we can expect revelation to accompany it.

A subtle, master tactic of the devil is to try to convince God's people that this kind of prayer ministry is only for specialists. The Bible does not even suggest that to become an intercessor one must be specially gifted.

Jesus Christ, as Son of man, came among us to show us how to live. He alone is our role model. And He modeled prayer as a daily priority for everyone.

The life of the Lord Jesus also clearly shows us the link between the ministry of intercession and the subsequent revelation that produces a deep understanding of people's needs. The Lord Jesus is undoubtedly the most effective and faithful (but probably the least thanked) intercessor for all of us. *"...he always lives to intercede for them"* (Hebrews 7:25b). Because of this, He fully understands us. *"Behold, God is mighty, and does not despise any; he is mighty in strength of understanding"* (Job 36:5 RSV). Therefore, the quickest way to understand the love of God for a nation, a race, a people group, a denomination, an organization, or an individual is to become an intercessor for them.

Let us look into the Scriptures and see how intercession is frequently linked with God-given revelation to people who made it a way of life.

Moses, the greatest intercessor in the Old Testament, had the greatest revelation of the glory of God.

Daniel, the man who prayed three times daily, was given remarkable revelation of present and future events.

Anna, the prophetess, who *"...never left the temple but worshiped night and day, fasting and praying"* (Luke 2:37b), was given the revelation that the baby in Mary's arms was the promised Messiah.

Cornelius is described in Acts 10 as a man who prayed constantly to God. One day while praying at three o'clock in the afternoon, an angel gave him direction to go and get Peter and bring him to his house.

Peter undoubtedly made prayer a way of life as we find him praying at noon while waiting for lunch to be prepared. (These two men of prayer were given the startling revelation that the gospel was for the Gentiles as well as for the Jews.)

Paul, the greatest intercessor in the New Testament (apart from the Lord Jesus), was given tremendous revelation of the Church Universal as well as revelations that were "not lawful to utter" (2 Corinthians 12:4). He wasn't permitted by God to share them.

God's character and His ways have not changed. God shares His secrets today with people whose hearts and motives are pure and who frequently intercede for others. To illustrate, here are extracts from a letter I received from the YWAM Director in Herare, Zimbabwe:

> During February, at our School of Evangelism, some people in one of our intercession groups received detailed revelation after carefully applying the Principles for Effective Intercession that you taught.
>
> To one was given the impression that he was to intercede for a man called Emmanuel de Costa; to another, that this man was in trouble with the police over drugs. Another had a vision of a man with a brief-case, standing on a dock in a port city.
>
> Understanding was then given to this group that this man was smuggling drugs and being arrested by the police.
>
> They prayed earnestly that he would repent of sin and commit his life to the Lord. Then they took authority over the powers of darkness on his behalf, in the name of the Lord Jesus Christ. Lastly, prayer was specifically made that someone would minister to him and lead him to the Lord. They believed God for his conversion.
>
> During our Southern Africa field trip through Zimbabwe, Malawi, Mozambique, Swaziland, South Africa and Botswana, we spent three weeks in

Mozambique (in June), of which ten days were spent in Lourenco Marques working with a drug rehabilitation center. One of the Christian workers named Mike worked with us as an interpreter. During one of our times in group intercession, Mike was impressed by the Holy Spirit to tell us that his real name was not Mike but Emmanuel de Costa. To our wonderment and excitement, we found that every detail God had revealed to us in intercession matched this man's life in February.

Can you imagine what that did to our faith?

Two weeks ago he and three other Christians were arrested by the Frelimo Government—this time not for being involved with drugs, but for sharing their faith in Christ, which was in direct conflict with the policy of the new government.

The four of them were subsequently released and have since continued to spread the good news of God's redeeming love. God has uniquely used this method of giving revelation to small intercession groups in YWAM worldwide as a powerful missions strategy.

Here's another example: People in prayer groups in YWAM both in Indonesia and in Brazil have been given specific revelation from the Holy Spirit about remote groups of people unreached by the gospel message. This has resulted in small trail-blazing teams going into remote areas in these countries dominated by satanic strongholds.

Pioneering teams, then church-planting teams, follow in time. The most radical pioneering missionary of all time said: *"...I will build my church, and the gates of Hades will not overcome it"* (Matthew 16:18b). Jesus continually proves the electrifying truth of those words.

Have we become so impressed by the world's systems of strategizing that we fail to avail ourselves of the simple method of waiting on God, listening to His voice, praying out His thoughts, and obeying what the master strategist says?

A young Hebrew alien in captivity once said, *"...there is a God in heaven who reveals mysteries" (Daniel 2:28a).* Because he believed it and sought God's face diligently, God rewarded him with His secrets.

SUGGESTED PRAYER

Dear God,

I want to know You more and hear Your voice more clearly so that I too can partner with You in meeting human needs through the wonderful ministry of praying for others.

Thank You that because You have given me this desire, You will fulfill it as I walk in obedience to truth. I anticipate a new dimension of revelation by the Holy Spirit in my praying for others.

In Jesus' name, Amen.

3

Praying for Our Friends

"Where in the world were you between four o'clock and four fifteen on [I named the day]? And what was happening to you?" I asked my friend Loren Cunningham at a leadership conference in Japan. Loren did some quick calculating and recalled that he was flying near the Philippines at the time. He described how suddenly the plane began to lose altitude very rapidly. It was as though the plane had lost all power and it was obvious to everyone on board that the pilots were having major problems controlling it.

The other passengers displayed understandable apprehension and couldn't hide their raw fear. In direct contrast, Loren was enveloped in a blanket of peace. The tension lasted several more minutes. Then the power returned, and the pilots regained control—to everyone's great relief.

I explained to Loren that at the exact time of the incident, thoughts of him had flashed across my mind. I had learned long ago to take seriously persistent impressions that related to my friends. God was probably alerting me to pray for them.

I started to pray for God to meet the needs of Loren's mind, body, soul, and spirit. The more I prayed, the more I became aware that Loren was in a difficult and dangerous situation. My prayers gained intensity as I asked God to send angelic protection, and I engaged in spiritual warfare against the powers of darkness. I prayed that whatever the circumstances, God would give Loren His supernatural peace, direction, and wisdom—and that Loren would come through completely unharmed. I prayed until I felt the burden lift.

At times I've been on the receiving end of this kind of prayer. On one occasion, my dear friend from Louisiana, Carolyn Alsup, awakened before day, praying for me. This is not unusual. Carolyn has been following my traveling and teaching schedule closely for many years so that she can intercede effectively.

On this particular occasion, as she was getting ready for church, the burden to pray for me returned to her. She sensed the need to engage in spiritual warfare against the enemy on my behalf. Still the burden persisted. Finally she told God she would not stop praying until He gave her a scripture assuring her of my safety. God honored her persistency and directed her to Psalm 118:17 "*[She (Joy)] will not die but live, and will proclaim what the* LORD *has done,*" which she repeated until she felt at peace.

Only God knows what plans of the enemy were derailed through Carolyn's prayer vigil. There are occasions when praying for another's protection can forestall a serious enemy attack. How I thank God for my faithful intercessor friend and for God's protection.

It's very meaningful to be able to partner with God through intercession for the needs of our friends. People have often said to me, "I couldn't get you out of my mind all day." If the purpose of the repeated impressions was for a prayer alert, and that had been discharged, the focus of their thoughts could have been redirected hours earlier. And it doesn't necessitate anyone being in danger, for the Holy Spirit to bring someone to our remembrance for intercession. The purposes could include any number of reasons for prayer.

God-given friendships are among our most treasured gifts. God has shown us ways in His Word to handle them with care. If we neglect them, it will be to our detriment. They are not easily replaced. "*To him who is afflicted, kindness should be shown by his friend*" (Job 6:14a NKJV). Kindness starts with intercession.

The Bible contains important implications both from successes and from failures in relation to praying for our friends who are going through difficult times.

SUCCESSES

Since Jesus is our role model, let's first look at Him for instruction on how to pray for our friends. How did Jesus relate to Peter, who was one of His closest friends when He was on earth? The ultimate Friend, Jesus prayed for Peter during his time of severe testing. "*Simon, Simon, Satan has asked to sift you as wheat*. But I have prayed for you, Simon, *that your faith may not fail*" [emphasis added](Luke 22:31–32a).

I believe that Jesus interceded to the Father on Peter's behalf so that Peter's faith in the character of God would not fail under the pressure of satanic buffeting. The devil is always trying to distort the character of God to everyone—particularly during times of difficulty and sorrow, and following failure. Because of Jesus' intercession for His friend Peter, repentance and restoration of fellowship came quickly after Peter's denial of his Lord.

The early disciples had learned how to pray from Jesus. They prayed earnestly for their friend Peter, and went without sleep when he was in prison. A dramatic escape with an angelic escort in the middle of the night was the result (Acts 12:7–11). Are we prepared to pay a similar cost when our friends are in difficult circumstances? We are to always pray for the seemingly impossible, and never limit God's ability or minimize the effectiveness of our prayers.

Moses interceding for Aaron, his brother and partner in leadership, is another illustration. Aaron had made the golden calf for the people to worship and God had pronounced the judgment of death on him: "*And the* LORD *was angry enough with Aaron to destroy him, but at that time I prayed for Aaron too*" (Deuteronomy 9:20). As a result,

Aaron's life was spared. We must never underestimate the possibility of a reversal of God's judgment through our intercession for a leader or a friend. I know of no more awesome role. It happened in the Word of God, and it has happened since, numbers of times.

I have often wondered what would have happened if Joshua or Caleb had interceded for Moses after God had pronounced judgment on him (Deuteronomy 3:26; 32:50–51). We have no record of anyone playing the role of an intercessor for Moses, as he had done for others. That's sad.

Job learned the importance of praying for his friends after they had misjudged him and failed to pray for him. He had to forgive them and intercede for God's mercy to be released to them. When he did, God gave him twice as much as he had possessed before he had lost everything.

God's intercession alerts today can come in unusual ways and at irregular times. By heeding them, we partner with God in some interesting adventures of turning potential tragedies into triumphs.

My friends, Len and Martha Ravenhill from Texas, were awakened one midnight by three distinct knocks on their closed bedroom door. Len got up, put on his slacks, and opened the door, but no one was there. He felt impressed to pray for his three sons, one at a time, who were in various parts of the world. He prayed for their protection and for divine intervention. At four a.m., exactly the same thing happened. Again Len prayed fervently for his three sons and their families—until he was at peace that whatever they were facing, God was intervening.

Understanding of this nocturnal happening came to this veteran intercessor (since deceased), when a letter arrived from his son David, who lived in Southern California. On exactly the same night that Len and Martha had been awakened, David and his wife Nancy were awakened at midnight with the noise from several fire trucks and firemen putting out a fire in the house next door. When they saw that the fire was under control, they went back to bed and to sleep.

At four a.m., they were awakened by someone knocking on their front door. When they opened it, a nice-looking man told them about a fire in the house next door that was now raging out of control. The stranger urged them to get out of their house, as the tops of the trees that separated them from their neighbor were already burning. David called the fire department while Nancy grabbed their baby and the man carried their four year-old daughter. As they walked across the street to safety, Nancy looked up into the dark sky and to her amazement saw a sentence written in red: "Your house will be saved."

The fire trucks were delayed in coming, and it looked impossible to save the house. While David tried desperately to get help from the neighbors, the stranger calmly announced to Nancy that no further help was needed. A police car then arrived and radioed for help, and finally the fire trucks came. In the nick of time, the house was saved.

David took their four-year-old daughter from the man who had been holding her. Then, just as David and Nancy were about to thank him for warning them about the danger, the man disappeared. He was nowhere to be seen. Shaken but profoundly grateful, the couple returned with their children to their unharmed home with a strong sense of the pervading presence of the Lord.

FAILURES

Let us learn now from those who failed to pray for their friends. Three of Job's friends failed Job in his darkest and most distressing hours.

"When Job's three friends, Eliphaz the Temanite, Bildad the Shuhite and Zophar the Naamathite, heard about all the troubles that had come upon him, they set out from their homes and met together by agreement to go and sympathize with him and comfort him. When they saw him from a distance, they could hardly recognize him; they began to weep aloud, and they tore their robes and sprinkled dust on their heads. Then they sat on the ground with him for seven days and seven nights. No one

said a word to him, because they saw how great his suffering was" (Job 2:11–13).

I paraphrase it this way: "They looked shocked, wailed loudly, ripped their clothes, were a dirty mess, stared at Job, and communicated nothing." It was enough to give him carbuncles as well as boils!

These friends' strange reaction wouldn't have helped Job one iota. If they had interceded for Job during his trials, they would have been in a position to receive understanding from God and to know whether they were to give Job counsel and, if so, of what nature. This would have kept them from giving the wrong counsel. Instead, they said that the cause of Job's problems was undealt-with sin, thereby judging him wrongly and adding to his distress.

If these friends had interceded, God's purposes for Job's life could have been accelerated. Obedience to the command *"Bear one another's burdens, and so fulfill the law of Christ"* (Galatians 6:2 NKJV) means involvement, starting with intercession.

HOW TO PRAY

The following are some "how-to"s when praying for friends who are going through trials:

1. Ask God for His miraculous intervention in our friends' circumstances. *"I am the LORD, the God of all mankind. Is there anything too hard for me?"* (Jeremiah 32:27).

2. Ask God to be glorified to the maximum in their lives. God's ultimate goal for every believer is to be more conformed to the image of His Son (Romans 8:29). Pray that our friends will recognize and desire this above all else. Ask God to pour out His abundant grace upon them and that, in turn, they will continue to receive it by faith. *"And I will do whatever you ask in my name, so that the Son may bring glory to the Father"* (John 14:13).

3. Ask God to show us what He's trying to teach *us* through our friends' trials, and give Him time to speak.

4. Thank God for the blessings received through our friends, *"...with thanksgiving, present your requests to God"* (Philippians 4:6).

5. We ask God to show us whether there's anything in our hearts that would hinder our prayers from being effective for them.

6. We ask God to fill us with His love for our friends, and receive His love by faith. "*God has poured out his love into our hearts by the Holy Spirit, whom he has given us*" (Romans 5:5b); "*...faith expressing itself through love*" (Galatians 5:6b).

7. We ask God to reveal Himself to our friends in the following ways:

   a. With a greater revelation of His character, especially His unfathomable love, absolute justice, limitless power, infinite understanding, and unswerving faithfulness. "*He is the Rock, his works are perfect, and all his ways are just. A faithful God who does no wrong, upright and just is he*" (Deuteronomy 32:4).

   We pray that through their suffering and perplexity, our friends will not lose faith in God's character. Ask God to infuse them with His faith to trust Him where they cannot trace Him. "*Who among you fears the* Lord *and obeys the word of his servant? Let him who walks in the dark, who has no light, trust in the name of the* Lord *and rely on his God*" (Isaiah 50:10).

   b. With a greater understanding of His ways. We pray that our friends will believe that God's delays are not necessarily His denials, and that they will come to the rest of faith by believing and appropriating the following truths:

   "*Now to him who is able to do immeasurably more than all we ask or imagine, according to his power that is at work within us*" (Ephesians 3:20); "*Commit your way to the* Lord; *trust in him, and he will act*" (Psalm 37:5 RSV).

   We pray that our friends will be encouraged by seeing the trial of their faith in light of God's big picture, since God sees the end from the beginning (2 Corinthians 4:16–18).

8. We ask God to reveal to them the utmost importance of maintaining a life of vocal praise and worship to Him. Nothing will better keep their spirits above the weight of their suffering, keep their minds at peace, enhance their intimacy of relationship with the Lord, and give them assurance that God is being glorified.

9. We ask God to draw our friends by His Spirit to regularly read the Bible and that as they do, He will quicken to them comforting and encouraging scriptures on which they can build their faith. "*Your statutes are my delight; they are my counselors*" (Psalm 119:24); "*This is my comfort in my affliction that thy promise gives me life*" (Psalm 119:50 RSV); "*If your law had not been my delight, I would have perished in my affliction*" (Psalm 119:92).

10. We ask God to stir our friends to ask Him the million-dollar question: "What is it you are trying to teach me?" and to persist in prayer until they know that God has spoken. Ask God to reveal to them the purposes and the causes of their difficulties.

11. We ask God to keep them from presuming upon His answers because of past experience, or what others might say. "*Keep back thy servant also from presumptuous sins; let them not have dominion over me!*" (Psalm 19:13a RSV).

12. We ask God to meet our friends' deepest needs and thank Him that He will.

13. We stand against the powers of darkness and command them to be driven back from our friends in the name of the Lord Jesus Christ and on the authority of His Word (James 4:7).

14. We need to communicate love to our friends, and that we're praying for them. Ask God to show us any practical ways to help them, and obey His promptings.

It was a cold winter's evening in January 1988. Jim had just come home from ten days in the hospital, having undergone serious and complicated open-heart surgery. The doorbell rang. When I opened the front door of my home in Southern California, I could hardly believe my eyes. No one was there, but an array of five beautifully prepared and packaged meals sat on the door step for Jim and me. I learned later that my much loved and close friend, Virginia Otis, had taken great effort to buy a special recipe book and cook a variety of meals consistent with Jim's prescribed, strict, low fat diet. Virginia had traveled for nearly an hour, and then turned around and driven home again after dropping off the food. She knew that I had hardly left Jim's side night and day and sensed that I needed practical help. That act of kindness and great thoughtfulness by this seasoned intercessor deeply ministered to me during our time of trial.

Very practical and meaningful deeds of kindness can flow out of intercession.

Six years later, this truth was remarkably demonstrated through our precious daughter Jill's sacrificial love. During my prolonged and very painful illness following back surgery in February 1994, when healing didn't come as expected, Jill's fervent and frequent intercession was matched only by her twenty-one months of meal preparations for us. Words are totally inadequate to describe the depths of my gratitude. Only God can justly reward her.

15. We ask God whether there's anything He wants us to send our friends either from His Word, or a taped teaching, or book, or gift. Then, if He does, we follow through in obedience as to the method and timing that He reveals. Don't presume anything.

During the time of my illness to which I have just referred, tremendous encouragement came from several women friends and from my daughter Jill, who diligently sought God on my behalf and received scriptural direction that I would eventually be healed. God's confirmation to Jim and me of their messages of hope, coupled with the other promises God had quickened to us from His Word, was like a lifeline during my darkest hours of trial and testing.

Many other dear friends continued to send me loving, encouraging letters. Some of them assured me that God had given them a similar, deep conviction for my healing during their numerous times of intercession. Some sent printed materials and taped teachings that were exactly what I needed to inspire and further encourage me. Others sent needed financial assistance. There is no price tag too high to evaluate the benefits that come to a suffering soul by such communicated love.

The fervent, consistent prayers of all our beloved family members, treasured, committed intercessor friends, and a host of other precious brothers and sisters in Christ around the world helped enormously to release the tide of God's grace needed to carry us through the long period of testing, refining, and reshaping through suffering and confinement.

While healing didn't come when expected, we were very encouraged and deeply ministered to, and our faith to endure was greatly strengthened. Our gratitude to these people cannot be measured or adequately expressed, but we regularly pray that God will reveal it to them, and administer the appropriate rewards.

At the time of completing this book in 1997, I can testify that while I am still in the fiery trial (improved but not yet healed), I am confident that God will deliver me when His many purposes are completed. *"He considered him faithful who had made the promise"* (Hebrews 11:11b).

I bow in worship, adoration, and praise to the Lover of my soul who is perfect in His character and ways. *"The* Lord *will fulfill his purpose for me"* (Psalm 138:8a).

From the early days of my severe pain, God led me to make a list of suffering friends' names and to make them among my top priority prayer projects. In fact, for months when I was too ill to do much else, my intercession focused almost solely on them. Suffering friends have become a continued emphasis in my prayer life.

Peter, James, and John missed the unique opportunity and privilege of praying for their friend Jesus during His greatest time of need in the Garden of Gethsemane. They failed Jesus. The result was that shortly afterwards, Peter denied his Lord three times. All forsook Him and fled.

Praying for our friends in their times of need can keep us from succumbing to temptation. *"Watch and pray so that you will not fall into temptation"* (Matthew 26:41a).

16. We must be sure to move from hope to faith each time we pray. God hears prayer, but answers faith. Praise Him that He is doing something that is consistent with His almightiness and His flawless character.

17. We shouldn't give up applying these principles when answers are delayed. That's when our friends more desperately need our continued prayers and encouragement.

I share this point from personal experience. The deepest appreciation flows from my heart for the number of dear friends who have persisted in intercession for me, and for those who have continued to communicate God-directed encouragement during this illness (over four and a half years to date). Some have fasted and prayed for me without seeing the desired and expected recovery. Undaunted, these close friends continue to pray and believe with me for it. My indebtedness to all in these categories is matched only by my gratitude and intercession for them. *"But as for you, be strong and do not give up, for your work will be rewarded"* (2 Chronicles 15:7).

I highly recommend Bob Sorge's insightful book, *The Fire of Delayed Answers*[1] for those who are going through prolonged trials. This book is in a class of its own.

SUGGESTED PRAYER

Dear God,

Thank You with all my heart for the wonderful gifts of friendship You have given me over a lifetime. Please alert me by Your Spirit to those in special need, both in sustained intercession and in practical ways. Increase my understanding of my privileges and responsibilities in prayer on their behalf. Thank You that You will.

In Jesus' name, Amen.

---

1. New York: Oasis House, 1996

4

How to Pray for Someone Near You Who Is Away from God

A fter I had finished speaking at a church in Northern California, a woman introduced herself and her husband to me and told me the following story.

This woman had earnestly prayed for many years for her husband's conversion, always asking God to move upon her husband and motivate him to come to church with her. As a keen church member, she found much joy and fulfillment in being involved in the life and ministry of her vital church. A part of that vitality was that people were regularly committing their lives to the Lord Jesus Christ during services, and the woman repeatedly thought, "If only my husband would come to church, I *know* he would be converted." The woman was disappointed and very puzzled as to why her prayers were not being answered. Her husband chose not to go to church and remained unconverted.

The woman had taken home a number of taped messages that I had given at her church the previous year, and she enthusiastically told her husband about their contents— always hoping and praying that he would come to church and hear these truths for himself.

One day the woman's husband amazed her by announcing that he had totally given his life to the Lord Jesus while at home by himself. He had listened to a series of my taped messages on divine guidance—while she was attending church! He said he wanted to experience friendship and fulfillment with God as He was described on those tapes.

The woman's husband then testified to me of an exciting walk with the Lord on a daily basis—seeking Him, listening to His voice, and obeying Him. The major lesson the woman said she learned was that by dictating to God the method He should use to accomplish her husband's conversion (that is, attending church with her), she had unwittingly hindered the process.

My next statement has no connection with the woman to whom I have just referred. God has a special word of instruction to wives of unconverted husbands in 1 Peter 3:1. He emphasizes the power that is released to influence their husbands to become Christians through the Christlike *living* of their wives, as opposed to their repeated preaching.

PURITY OF MOTIVE

Another major hindrance to answered prayer when praying for someone we love who is away from God is having an impure motive. So many times, our main reason for wanting people to be converted is that life would be so much easier for *us* if they were Christians.

We need to ask God to purify our *motives* so that our requests for the souls of our loved ones to be saved come from a genuine, deep desire for God to be glorified to the maximum regardless of the cost to us, or to them. When we start praying that kind of prayer, we find we are soon tested. Those who understand God's character will pass the tests.

LESSONS WE NEED TO LEARN

As we submit to the Person of the Holy Spirit and obey His promptings, we will find that He puts the focus on us first. God wants us to say to Him, "What is it You are trying to teach me? I want to learn those lessons more than I want my circumstances to be changed."

We can then say, "If more glory can come to Your name by delaying the answers to my prayers, that's fine with me. Do whatever is needed in my life to bring me to the place where I have maximum effectiveness when I pray for those who are lost."

Now those are the people who mean business with God. And those are the people with whom God does business.

TOTAL RELINQUISHMENT

With a passionate desire for God to be glorified we will say with Paul, *"I eagerly expect and hope that I will in no way be ashamed, but will have sufficient courage so that now as always Christ will be exalted in my body, whether by life or by death"* (Philippians 1:20). We continue to say, "If by my death these unconverted people could be brought to You, I'm a candidate for death. Their soul's salvation means more to me than life." That is total relinquishment of oneself.

Then comes total relinquishment of the unconverted people, which also deals with selfish motives. We pray, "If more glory can come to Your name by Your bringing lost ones to You and then immediately taking them to heaven, that's also fine with me."

When we truly have a burdened heart for the lostness of people's souls, we will pray, "God, do anything that is required to bring them to the end of themselves—even if that means illness or injury, temporary or permanent." Are we prepared for these implications?

God both desires and has the power to bring us to the place where our desire for people to be in a right relationship with Him is greater than our desire for their—or our own—physical well-being.

Are we prepared to say to God, "Use anyone, anywhere, under any circumstances, to bring that lost soul to You"? Or have we prejudices (maybe hidden ones) about whom we would *not* want God to use?

We also need to relinquish the unconverted to God in relation to their future. We need to pray, "Lord, if after their conversion You should call them to a foreign mission field or they are martyred for You and I face the possibility of never seeing them again, that's okay. They're in Your hands for the present and the future."

TESTINGS RELATED TO GOD'S GLORY

We may have already said the foregoing to God but never really relinquished the people nearest and dearest to us into His hands, so that by their death, if necessary, God could use this to bring the unconverted to Himself. That's really where we know beyond a shadow of a doubt that we're praying one hundred percent for God's glory and have a God-given burden for the lost souls for whom we're praying. That's taking our Isaacs and laying them upon the altar on Mount Moriah. I know. I've been there! It's the ultimate test, because we know that God can take us at our word and we can be left widowed or childless or friendless or orphaned.

We can pray like this only if we understand the character of the One to whom we are praying. That understanding comes through studying God's character facet by facet from His Word, and being obedient to revealed truth.

God will never do anything inconsistent with His character. He is absolutely righteous and just, infinite in His knowledge and wisdom, unsearchable in His understanding, and unfathomable in His love. Because of *who He is* we can trust Him—to act according to the highest good for all concerned.

RELEASE FROM FEAR

We can fear dying ourselves, and we can fear our loved ones' dying. But when we really relinquish ourselves and our loved ones to God and truly want the greatest glory to come to His name through each of those lives, I can assure you that all fear leaves us, and God's peace takes its place.

If God decides to answer our prayers in the ways that we have released Him to, we can expect Him to do such wonderful things as a result of the people's conversions that the joy will outweigh the sorrow that has accompanied the sacrifice.

"The Lord is just in all his ways, and kind in all his doings" (Psalm 145:17 RSV). We can also believe God to heal our broken heart and bind up our wounds (Psalm 147:3).

As we pass these tests by God's grace and with the understanding of His flawless character, not only are our motives for praying purified, but God brings us into closer friendship with Himself.

THE IMPORTANCE OF RIGHT ATTITUDES

The nearer we get to God, the more we become aware that our attitudes toward the people for whom we are praying are all-important for the further release of God's power through us. So often, the people whom we love but who are far away from God are those who have hurt us deeply. We need to make sure that we feel no resentment toward them as we pray for them. It is possible to pray fervently and for many years for people we have never forgiven. This is a major hindrance to our prayers being answered. *"See to it that no one misses the grace of God and that no bitter root grows up to cause trouble and defile many"* (Hebrews 12:15).

Perhaps we know the truth of this all too well, but still struggle to forgive. The following nine practical steps will produce sure forgiveness if diligently taken:

1. Realize that forgiveness is an act of the will. We have to want to forgive.

2. Understand that resentment is destructive to the mind, body, soul, and spirit. *"A tranquil mind gives life to the flesh, but passion makes the bones rot"* (Proverbs 14:30 RSV).

3. Realize that we will not be forgiven by God unless we forgive others who have hurt us. *"And when you stand praying, if you hold anything against anyone, forgive him, so that your Father in heaven may forgive you your sins"* (Mark 11:25).

4. Think of all that God has forgiven us. *"Be kind and compassionate to one another, forgiving each other, just as in Christ God forgave you"* (Ephesians 4:32); *"As the Lord has forgiven you, so you also must forgive"* (Colossians 3:13b RSV). God forgives us instantly, joyfully, and wholly.

5. Thank the Lord for any or all of the blessings He has brought to us through the people who have hurt us.

6. Think of the needs—mental, physical, emotional, and spiritual—of the individuals at the time of their hurting us. Their needs then—and now—are probably greater than ours.

7. We ask God to give us His supernatural ability to love and forgive those people. Acknowledge that this is the work of the Holy Spirit and receive it by faith. *"God has poured out his love into our hearts by the Holy Spirit, whom he has given us"* (Romans 5:5b); *"And without faith, it is impossible to please God"* (Hebrews 11:6a). Galatians 5:6 says that *"faith [expresses] itself through love."* And God has promised in 1 Corinthians 13:8a that *"love never fails."*

8. We ask God for opportunities to express His love to these people both in word and in deed. *"If anyone has material possessions and sees his brother in need but has no pity on him, how can the love of God be in him? Dear children, let us not love with words or tongue but with actions and in truth"* (1 John 3:17–18).

9. Become a regular intercessor for them. Pray for God to bless them, encourage them, comfort them, strengthen them, and meet their deepest needs. *"But I tell you: Love your enemies and pray for those who persecute you"* (Matthew 5:44).

A dedicated Christian woman in California told me that after she had heard me speak on the subject of forgiveness, the Holy Spirit convicted her of her long-standing resentment toward her son-in-law.

Her son-in-law was unconverted, and for years had been cruel to her daughter and her grandchildren, causing her much sorrow. She had prayed fervently for years for his conversion, but without results.

That same night at 11:30 p.m., the woman knelt beside her bed and repented of her resentment. She then applied every one of the preceding nine steps as she realized the cause for the ineffectiveness of her prayers for her son-in-law's conversion. It was a Thursday night.

The following Saturday morning, her son-in-law unexpectedly burst into her house. He announced the startling news that at exactly 11:30 p.m. on the previous Thursday night he had felt a strong conviction of sin, had repented, and had given his life to Christ. He said that he had asked forgiveness of his wife and children and that he had felt compelled to drive to her home (although a long distance away) to ask for her forgiveness for all the heartache he had caused her. As soon as the woman had forgiven her son-in-law, God was able to answer her prayers.

RELEASE OF POWER THROUGH HUMBLING OURSELVES

We need to be encouraged that the more we let God work on us, the more the power of His Spirit will be released to work through us as we pray for the lost. Humbling ourselves before God and the people for whom we're praying is a strong factor in releasing that power.

We should ask God to show us any areas in our lives where we might have tempted the unconverted to rebel against Him. Even if we were ignorant of our doing so at the time, we still need to confess and make restitution as God directs.

It is also important to tell ourselves and them that we believe that God is greater in love, mercy, and power than our mistakes. *"Consecrate yourselves, for tomorrow the Lord will do amazing things among you"* (Joshua 3:5b).

So much of people's lack of commitment to the Lord Jesus is due to their warped view of the character of God. If we have in any way contributed to that distortion, whether by ignorance, or disobedience to revealed truth, we need to acknowledge it to those people—explaining which facets of God's character were misrepresented by our lives. *"This is the one I esteem: he who is humble and contrite in spirit, and trembles at my word"* (Isaiah 66:2b). Our broken and contrite spirits are a powerful factor that God uses to help bring about contrition in those for whom we are praying.

FASTING AND PRAYER

Since fasting and prayer are often linked together in Scripture with powerful results, we need to be obedient to God's promptings in this regard. Always remember that it's not our fasting that impresses God, only our obedience. The young women at a YWAM School of Evangelism in Switzerland where I was teaching were directed one day by God to fast and pray throughout the day for their unconverted brothers. Remarkable results followed, as some of the girls soon heard about their brothers' conversions.

We can expect to be prompted by the Holy Spirit at times to fast and pray concerning special burdens God puts upon our hearts. In Matthew 6:6 Jesus said, "*...when you pray,*" in verse 2 He said, "*...when you give*" and in verses 16 and 17 He said, "*...when you fast.*" Jesus' repeated use of the word "when" implies that praying, giving, and fasting are acts of obedience that Jesus requires of his disciples.

SPIRITUAL WARFARE

The Bible makes it very clear in 1 John 5:19b (RSV) that the "*whole world is in the power of the evil one,*" but Jesus said, "*I have overcome the world*" (John 16:33b), and God's power is infinitely greater than Satan's. This means that when we pray for the lost, we need to take our stand against the enemy regularly, and command him in the all-powerful name of the Lord Jesus Christ to retreat from them and loose his grip from their spirits, minds, souls, and bodies.

Quote the Word of God, which is our sword in spiritual warfare. The following verses are very powerful as we exercise faith in the power of the written Word:

"*The reason the Son of God appeared was to destroy the devil's work*" (1 John 3:8b).

"*And they overcame [Satan] by the blood of the Lamb, and by the word of their testimony; and they loved not their lives unto the death*" (Revelation 12:11 KJV).

"*I will build my church; and the gates of hell shall not prevail against it*" (Matthew 16:18b KJV).

"...*whatever you bind on earth will be bound in heaven, and whatever you loose on earth will be loosed in heaven*" (Matthew 18:18b).

We must always realize that no matter how difficult or how seemingly hopeless or resistant the unconverted people are, we are not fighting them. We are fighting the enemy, who is our opponent. "*For we wrestle not against flesh and blood, but against the principalities, against powers, against the rulers of the darkness of this world, against spiritual wickedness in high places*" (Ephesians 6:12 KJV).

Satan doesn't give up his victims without a fight. Our warfare is often like a wrestling match. The victory is seldom won in the first round, or necessarily in the second or third. Persistence is necessary in order to win.

We need to constantly remind Satan that "*greater is he [the Lord Jesus] that is in [us] than he that is in the world [the devil]*" (1 John 4:4b KJV). "Therefore," let us tell him, "someone has to lose in this battle, and it's not going to be us." Declare this in faith enough times, and the devil will start believing you and will finally give up. That's been my experience, anyway. I have told Satan that while ever there is breath in my body, I'll fight him by the power and strength of the Holy Spirit for the lost souls for whom I'm particularly burdened, so he might as well quit now. We can then ask God to frustrate Satan's plans in the lives of the people for whom we are praying, and then believe for divine intervention.

THE REVELATION OF GOD'S CHARACTER

Next we should pray that God will reveal to the lost souls the absolute reasonableness of surrendering their wills to the Lord Jesus by giving them understanding of His character. Only God knows of which facets of His character the unsaved have a distorted view. Ask God to use any means to correct that distortion, and believe that He will.

Ask God to reveal Himself to them in personal ways that they cannot refute, and bring them to the realization that by becoming a Christian they have everything to gain and nothing to lose. Follow this closely by praying that God will bring them to an end of themselves, that everything they are doing to pursue fulfillment outside the pursuit of Him will turn sour and only produce frustration and emptiness. We don't need to make suggestions to the One who is ingenious in His creativity and infinite in His wisdom and knowledge. He has limitless ways that we have neither heard, nor thought of, to answer our prayers.

Now we can ask God to put the fear of the Lord upon those lost souls and restrain them from evil. *"through the fear of the* LORD *a man avoids evil"* (Proverbs 16:6b). They can be in circumstances of strong temptation, but God can use our prayers to keep them from entering deeper into sin.

THE POWER OF THE WORD OF GOD

"The entrance of Your words gives light; it gives understanding to the simple" (Psalm 119:130 NKJV). We should therefore pray that God will bring His Word to the unsaved, or take them to His Word and give them a desire to read it. God has numerous ways of answering that prayer. Just believe that He will. Derek Prince, a doctor of philosophy, was converted without human instrumentality through reading the Word of God, and later became an international Bible teacher.

Some of the people for whom we are praying have been exposed to a lot of truth and have hardened their hearts to it. We need to cry out for God to release His mercy to them. Mercy is not getting what we deserve. Moses pleaded for God's mercy for the children of Israel and God answered his prayer. The Israelites' disobedience, rebellion, unbelief, and murmuring certainly deserved God's judgment, but Moses' prayers stayed God's hand of judgment and released His arm of mercy. It is an enormous privilege today to play the same role as an intercessor on behalf of those in similar condition of heart. We can pray, *"In wrath remember mercy"* (Habakkuk 3:2b).

THE PRAISE OF FAITH

To be praying at the deepest level of faith, we can ask God to quicken some Scriptures to us that will encourage us to keep on believing that He is working regardless of what we may or may not see. 2 Chronicles 6:30b says, *"...you know his heart (for you alone know the hearts of men)."*

God can see whether or not the people we are praying for are walking towards the Lord Jesus. He knows whether or not they are softening towards Him and desiring to turn away from their present way of living. If this is so, He will want to encourage us from His Word, as we seek Him. Consequently, it becomes easier for us to enter into the praise of faith. We picture these people as God will make them: "new creatures in Christ Jesus," filled with His love, manifesting the life of Christ. We then praise God wholeheartedly that He is working and that He will accomplish it.

A young woman who attended one of the schools of evangelism where I was teaching had been totally cut off by her parents because she had become a Christian. Her parents had ceased to communicate with her, and she had no idea where they were. She heard me teach on the praise of faith, which was powerfully quickened to her by the Holy Spirit. She began praising God daily in faith for her parents' salvation. Within weeks, her parents were marvelously converted and had made contact with her. Such is the power released through praise.

Since we don't know which of these prayer principles God will use to bring about the conversions of those for whom we pray, let's use them all.

There are times when we are particularly burdened for the welfare of the unconverted and the circumstances are outside of our control or ability to help them. To have peace of mind, we need to put Psalm 37:5 (RSV) into action: *"Commit your way to the Lord; trust in him, and he will act."* The Hebrew word for "commit" literally means "to throw." We "throw" the ones for whom we are concerned at God, asking only that He act to bring the greatest glory to His name in their circumstances.

God is all-powerful, has the knowledge of all that is knowable, has all wisdom, is totally righteous and just, and is all loving. Therefore, He has the ability to catch those we throw at Him, knows how to work on them for their best interests, knows the best methods and timing, will do only the right and just things by everyone concerned, and longs to catch them. Love's arms hate to be empty!! God then promises to act. We believe His Word. Miraculous peace follows.

GOD'S SOVEREIGNTY AND MAN'S FREE WILL

God has given man free will, and that is a fixed law that will not be violated. However, through our interceding according to God's ways, His hand is moved to bring influences and pressures to bear upon the people for whom we are praying.

As we persist in prayer and pray tenaciously like Jesus exhorts us to do in Luke 11:5–8 and 18:2–8, there comes a time when the unconverted find it easier to yield their lives to the Lord than to hold out against Him. This is what Elijah meant when he prayed for the fire to fall on the water-drenched altar on Mount Carmel in front of the prophets of Baal and the people of Israel. *"Answer me, O LORD, answer me, so these people will know that you, O LORD, are God, and that you are turning their hearts back again"* (1 Kings 18:37).

In Psalm 33:15 (RSV) the psalmist has the same thought when he says that God looks down from heaven and *"…fashions the hearts of them all, and observes all their deeds."* What an awesome privilege and opportunity to be able to cooperate with God in "fashioning the hearts of men" through the wonderful ministry of intercession.

Our spiritual ambition for the extension of God's kingdom will be manifest by the way in which we pray for the lost. We can be satisfied with praying just for their conversion, or we can pray that they will be converted and become deeply committed disciples of the Lord Jesus. We can pray that they will have a burning desire to know God and make Him known and impact their generation in the power of the Holy Spirit. We can pray that from their steps of obedience to revealed truth, they will be among the overcomers as described in the book of Revelation and be a part of the Bride of Christ.

You may be thinking, "I don't have enough of a burden for lost souls like you're describing to motivate me to pray to this extent." Dear reader, that's okay. But you can take hold of God and ask Him to give you that burden, and refuse to let Him go until He does.

Don't be discouraged if you don't receive a quick answer. You're asking for something of great value. God may test you to see how much you really want to share some of His heart for the lost. When He sees that it's of the utmost importance to you, He surely will answer you. And intimate friendship with God will increase.

GIVE GOD ALL THE GLORY

Finally, it is of paramount importance to tell God that when our prayers are answered, we understand that it wasn't our praying or our fasting or our diligence that caused the miracle of new birth in another. It was because of His grace, His mercy, His power, and His love. We need also to remind ourselves of the part others, perhaps many others, have played through prayer. *"Not to us, O Lord, not to us but to your name be the glory, because of your love and faithfulness"* (Psalm 115:1).

SUGGESTED PRAYER

Dear God,

Thank You for making it clear that no one is beyond the reach of Your unfathomable love and unending mercy. Enlarge my heart by making it more like Yours towards the lost. Increase my faith to persevere in prayer for those who are still resistant to You.

By Your grace, I choose to pay whatever price You ask, that precious lost souls may come into Your kingdom. Give them and me a far greater revelation of what You're really like. I believe that is our greatest need. Thank You that You will.

In Jesus' name, Amen.

For 10-16-05 Ch 5

1. What kind of choices are we faced with as we go deeper w/ prayer?

2. What is the price of intercession?

3. What can we learn fr. these people Abraham, Elijah etc?

4. P56-59 - what does speaking have to do w/ intercession?

$$\boxed{5}$$

How Far Will We Go?

*H*ow deep we go in prayer is entirely up to us. It depends on how seriously we want to take this privilege of praying for others. Many prefer to stay in the comfort zones of the shallow waters; others choose to launch out into the deep. Deep-sea fishing is costly in money, time, energy, and equipment. But it's much more exhilarating and rewarding. There's a lot of dynamic action. Only the really big fish are caught in the deeper waters.

Intercession can be like that—and so much more. It depends on how far we want God to take us. Make no mistake about it, there's a price; but it's far outweighed by the privileges and rewards.

WHAT WILL IT COST US?

Consider the following:

1. Time. Giving up doing other good, legitimate things. We have to decide to make intercession a priority.

2. Energy. Greater intensity of desire. It can involve weeping, groaning, travail of spirit, and fasting. *"And there is no one who calls on Your name, Who stirs himself up to take hold of You"* (Isaiah 64:7a NKJV).

3. Sleep. It was when the disciples did not stay awake that Jesus asked them, *"Could you men not keep watch with me for one hour?"* (Matthew 26:40b).

4. Purity of motive. Intercession is mostly done in secret. *"But when you pray, go into your room, close the door and pray to your Father, who is unseen. Then your Father, who sees what is done in secret, will reward you"* (Matthew 6:6).

5. Great faith. We seldom see results immediately. We may have to wait for years, or we may never see the answers. Therefore, intercession requires more faith than most other kinds of service.

Could it be that because of its great price, intercession is largely unpopular and neglected? *"I looked for a man among them who would build up the wall and stand before me in the gap on behalf of the land so I would not have to destroy it, but I found none"* (Ezekiel 22:30).

It is very significant to note God's reaction to men's choices in this regard. It is a strong reaction. Ponder these verses:

"He saw that there was no one, he was appalled that there was no one to intervene" (Isaiah 59:16a); *"I looked, but there was no one to help; I was appalled, but there was no one to uphold"* (Isaiah 63:5a RSV).

Why is God *appalled* at the lack of intercession? He has made it clear from Genesis to Revelation that prayer is the match that lights the fuse to release the explosive power of the Holy Spirit in the affairs of men. It's therefore reasonable to expect that God is at a loss to understand why we don't think intercession should be given priority time.

We can learn valuable lessons from biblical characters that will help us decide how far we'll go in intercession.

Abraham had a burdened heart for the cities of Sodom and Gomorrah, so much so that the Bible says that the outcry against the sin, and the subsequent concern for the judgment it would bring, got God's attention (Genesis 18:20).

When the angels had finished speaking to Abraham and were headed toward Sodom, Abraham *"remained standing before the* LORD" (verse 22). The first sign of wanting to go deeper is when the others have finished praying and your burdened heart wants to press further into God.

Abraham starts off boldly in his petition for God to spare the cities, presenting his case on the basis of the righteousness and justice of God's character. His highly commendable start, and subsequent conversation through to verse 30, then takes a different turn. Abraham suggests three times that God could be getting angry for his continuing requests to spare the cities because of relatively few righteous people in them, although nothing is coming from God that even hints of anger.

In verse 32, Abraham becomes timid and apologetic and finally terminates his conversation with God. The part that saddens me is that he asked God only six times to spare the cities. Seven is the number of completion in the Bible.

What if Abraham had asked God the seventh time to spare the people, if fewer than ten righteous people could be found? The outcome for Sodom and Gomorrah could possibly have been different. Was Abraham's understanding of the extent of God's mercy limited? The effect of our intercession for individuals, churches, cities and nations will depend upon two things:

1. How desperate we are for divine intervention.
2. How acquainted we are with the character of God.

Elijah's public prayer on Mt. Carmel for fire (a symbol of the power of God) to descend from heaven upon the wet wood before the prophets of Baal was answered. One short prayer; dramatic and immediate results!

The scenario is different when God wants to take the same man into deeper dimensions of prayer. A little later we find Elijah praying for rain. God wants to teach him what it means to press in and to hold on to God in prevailing prayer. He wants to enlarge Elijah's faith. Here we have a perfect picture of disciplined, desperate praying. *"So Ahab went off to eat and drink, but Elijah climbed to the top of Carmel, bent down to the ground and put his face between his knees"* (1 Kings 18:42).

No quick dramatic answers this time. When Elijah's servant reported that there was still no sign of rain after six times of looking toward the sea, we read *"Seven times Elijah said, 'Go back'"* (verse 43). Desperate praying with persistency finally paid off. What started with a cloud the size of a man's hand became a downpour that broke a three-and-a-half year drought.

Rain is a biblical symbol of the outpouring of the Holy Spirit in revival (Ezekiel 34:26; Joel 2:23), Revival praying requires intensity, tenacity, and persistency. There are no quick answers. When we have a God-given vision and burden for revival and spiritual awakening, *we pray until God answers.* Giving up is unthinkable! The darkest hours of spiritual decadence and dryness often come right before the dawn of God's sovereign deluges.

God entrusted **Elisha** with a strong prophetic ministry accompanied by remarkable miracles. It is significant that the greatest miracle required the greatest price in intercession. God's required involvement for Elisha as he ministered to the dead boy on his bed was private, personal, persistent, prevailing prayer—until life returned (2 Kings 4:32-35). What miracles of the spiritually and physically dead would God perform for us if we were prepared to go deeper and deeper in prayer for others?

I was walking off the platform of a large international, interdenominational conference where I had spoken, when a dear friend approached me. It was a joy to see her. She knew I had to leave that afternoon and fly to speak at another conference, so she wasted no time in sharing with me her grief stricken heart, which was etched all over her beautiful face. Her only son was dying of AIDS contracted while living a homosexual lifestyle. Her son lived in my part of the United States—Los Angeles. After praying for the woman under the direction of the Holy Spirit, I shared two things with her. I would bear her burden with her in prayer, and my son-in-law, John Bills (J. B.), who ministers to people dying with AIDS in Los Angeles, would be available to her son Curt in any way possible. Knowing this brought her great comfort. That was October.

During the ensuing three months, Curt's parents took turns flying from their home state to Southern California. We were in constant contact, acutely aware that the greatest battle was for Curt's immortal soul, as he was unconverted.

The weaker he became, the greater intensity we experienced in intercession. Curt responded favorably to our son-in-law's gentle, compassionate manner, and respected his wise but uncompromising approach to eternal issues. (It is important to relate here that Curt's loving, godly parents had prayed regularly for him since his infancy and had done their best to bring him up in the ways of God. Much fervent prayer had been made for Curt by his parents and by friends over the years, increasingly so in recent months and weeks.)

A medical report came that Curt's days were numbered. Because of the heavy medication due to the extreme pain he was suffering, there were only about two or, at the most, three times in twenty-four hours when Curt's mind was clear enough for anyone to carry on a meaningful conversation with him. Each conversation lasted about fifteen minutes. J. B. would try, whenever possible, to be with Curt during those times. On one such occasion, J. B. pointed out what the Bible clearly states with regard to homosexuality and pleaded with Curt to renounce his lifestyle in order that his soul could be saved (1 Corinthians 6:9–10; Revelation 21:8; 22:14–15).

Curt responded tenderly without a trace of bitterness, "You're the hound of heaven to me, but" he added, "I can't. It's too much a part of my life." Those words triggered a desperation in intercession at an even deeper level for Curt's mother and me. I experienced an agony of soul that I'm at a loss to adequately describe. It was as though I couldn't bear to go on living, knowing that my precious friend's son would be lost for eternity.

After months of fervent, persistent, faith-filled praying without an answer, I became aware that there had to be another dimension to prayer. Something was needed that would cause God to release the necessary revelation and conviction to Curt.

Never before had I been more acutely aware of how totally dependent we are on the Holy Spirit to produce revelation and I was puzzled as to why He hadn't yet done so. We'd asked for it so many times. Could it be that God's Spirit had ceased to strive with this young man? If He had, I could ask God to reconsider His verdict, as Moses had done on behalf of the children of Israel.

I pleaded for God to release the greatest extent of His mercy. I told God that I agreed with Him completely that because of the truth that Curt had known and had willfully rejected, God was absolutely just in all that had happened. Through my travail and tears, I pleaded with God as though my own life depended upon the answer, to give Curt *one more chance*.

The next morning while reading my Bible I asked God to speak to me if He had answered my prayers of the night before. Immediately He directed me to Jeremiah 16:21 (NKJV), *"Therefore behold, I will this once cause them to know, I will cause them to know My hand and My might; And they shall know that My name is the* LORD*"*.

I was awed by His answer. I asked whether there was anything else He wanted to say. Just as quickly, He directed me to Ezekiel 37. The understanding came that just as Ezekiel spoke to the dead bones in obedience and faith to God's directions and the bones came to life, if I were to speak Curt's name and vocalize my faith in God's ability to bring Curt's dead soul to spiritual life, God would do it. I did so forcefully, in full faith, according to God's living and all-powerful Word.

No sooner had I recorded the Scriptures in my diary than the phone rang. It was J. B. Curt's mother had phoned him to say that Curt had just requested for J. B. to come and see him. Curt had explained, "I have unfinished business with him."

My burden in prayer continued until I heard J. B.'s voice on the phone a few hours later saying, "Curt was fully conscious when I arrived. He was eager to share with me that some dark pages in his life's record needed to be removed. They represented his homosexual lifestyle, which he now wanted to renounce."

J. B. went on to say, "Over the past few hours, during intermittent times of consciousness, Curt made it very clear to me that he now agreed with God's Word and saw his need for true repentance. He repented fully and freely, declaring Jesus Christ as the Lord of his life. For the first time, it was evident that Curt had peace of mind."

I now wept with relief and unspeakable joy. Later, Curt's mother told me of some other factors that contributed to this dramatic change. Early in the day just described, Curt's mother had received a call from the night nurse saying that Curt wanted to see her. Curt was quick to share with his mother that he had experienced either a vision or a dream. In it, a hand appeared holding a book, and a voice said, "Curt this book is your life, and in it are some dark pages that need to be removed through repentance of sin."

Curt explained to his mother that he now understood what she and John Bills had been trying to tell him. He also understood that he no longer felt that he had to be attractive to men or to women. This understanding was accompanied by such a sense of freedom, that Curt kept repeating, "This must be a deliverance."

Curt died ten days later. Hours before he died, he saw a vision of heaven, and with outstretched arms and a radiant face, he kept repeating, "I'm ready to come to You, Jesus." Curt's physical eyes were blinded by AIDS, but his spiritual sight had never been clearer.

The grief of Curt's parents over losing their only son was understandably very deep, but their gratitude to God for His mercy was deeper. They and we embraced the truth: *"As for God, his way is perfect"* (Psalm 18:30a); *"O give thanks unto the LORD; for he is good: for his mercy endureth for ever"* (Psalm 136:1 KJV).

Is there any service for God that brings greater fulfillment than the wonderful ministry of intercession?

Moses is a classic example of an intercessor who went the full distance on behalf of others. After God had passed His judgment of annihilation on the children of Israel for their disobedience, unbelief, and murmuring, Moses was undeterred.

He dialogued with the Almighty according to what he knew of God's character, and manifested strong spiritual ambition for that character not to be distorted to God's enemies.

Moses reasoned with God that His character would be misjudged by the Egyptians if He kept to His plan. After all, the Egyptians had good reason to know how powerfully God had directed and delivered the Israelites against overwhelming odds from Pharoah's army. If God wiped out His people now, His enemies would think He didn't have what it takes to continue directing and protecting His people.

Then from his knowledge of God's character, Moses pressed another point. While fully acknowledging the seriousness of the Israelites' sins, Moses asked God to demonstrate even greater strength by a greater display of mercy and forgiveness to the undeserving rebels. And if this was not God's desire—and here Moses goes all the way—Moses says to God, "Blot me out of your book," meaning, "I'll take the punishment for their sin." This is the ultimate act of intercession. The high price Moses paid to have intimate friendship with God was rewarded by God's response. God said He would spare their lives but punish them for their sins. He sent a plague among them.

It is significant to note two things. First, Moses' great love for God and for the people he led was a reflection of the heart of the One with whom he had spent so much time alone. *"And we, who with unveiled faces all reflect the Lord's glory, are being transformed into his likeness with ever-increasing glory, which comes from the Lord, who is the Spirit"* (2 Corinthians 3:18). Moses' reactions to God reflected God's actions to men.

Second, this story is not recorded to intimidate us by Moses' experience as though we could never attain to such a lofty level of prayer. The very opposite is true. Any one of us can choose to study God's character and ways from His Word and live accordingly.

Any one of us can know God intimately through choosing to hate sin in thought, word and deed. It's called having the fear of the Lord (Proverbs 8:13). Any one of us can choose to make intercession a way of life. Any one of us can choose to obey the promptings of the Holy Spirit and be taken into the deeper waters of prayer for others. Any one of us can be used of God to alter the course of history.

God's invitation is clear. His promises of assured results are conclusive. *"Ask of me, and I will make the nations your inheritance, the ends of the earth your possession. You will rule them with an iron scepter; you will dash them to pieces like pottery"* (Psalm 2:8–9); *"Behold, I will make of you a threshing sledge, new, sharp, and having teeth; you shall thresh the mountains and crush them, and you shall make the hills like chaff"* (Isaiah 41:15 RSV).

Will we accept the invitation? Will we believe God's promises? How far are we willing to go in intercession?

SUGGESTED PRAYER

Dear Father God,

I acknowledge my need and desire to have an increased spiritual ambition to go deeper in prayer for others. I want to have a greater burden for lost souls. I want to be more sensitized to the promptings of the Holy Spirit when praying for others, and to be more fully obedient to Him.

I am willing to adjust my priorities to have more time with You so that I can have an increased understanding from Your Word of Your character and Your ways.

I now commit myself to do my part, and I submit to You in faith that You will work these things in and through me. Thank You that You will.

In Jesus' name, Amen.

See page 5 regarding ministries that are available for people who need others to partner with in prayer for serious personal needs.

6

Praying for This Generation of Suffering Youth and Children

A 17-year-old boy from Detroit gave three reasons why he robbed banks:

1. He might get away with the money.

2. He could be arrested and put in prison and be given a warm place to sleep and three meals a day.

3. He could be shot and killed and taken out of his misery. We all need to understand the pain behind that reasoning. I find my heart also hurting for God.

I often pause to marvel at His incomparable ability to function flawlessly in all dimensions of His character and personality, while at the same time coping with the excruciating suffering of seeing the accumulated pain of a fallen world.

I cannot comprehend it!

I can stop and worship Him.

I do.

Is it because the young are so helpless and vulnerable that God emphasizes the need to pray for them?

Is it because of God's strong commitment to justice while children are so often subjected to injustice?

Is it because they are more likely than adults to respond to the gospel?

Is it because this could well be the last generation of young people before the coming of the Lord?

Is it because Father God's compassionate heart hurts so deeply over children's pain?

Is it because God longs to remove the distorted views of Him that adults have given to children?

Is it because God yearns to reveal Himself to them as He really is?

Is it because God is lonely for children's friendship?

Is it because God just loves them, period?

I believe it's for all these reasons, and more, that God has allowed my heart (and others' hearts) to be broken repeatedly over our children's need to experience Jesus' healing love and life.

We can only be hurt to the extent that we love. Because God loves the most, He hurts the most—hurts when we grieve Him, act independently of Him, disbelieve Him and disobey Him. And then He hurts when we suffer the consequences.

But think of how He must hurt over the suffering of the helpless and the innocent.

God's purpose is not to make us sad when we see the hurting youth and children of the world, but to help us to become more like Him through entering into *"the fellowship of sharing in his sufferings"* (Philippians 3:10b). A sign of friendship with God is to keep asking Him to share with us the concerns closest to His heart. One of those concerns is undoubtedly the suffering youth and children of this messed up, fragmented world. As we intercede, the needs of the needy will be met, because God delights to go into action to answer the prayers of His close friends.

The meaning of Jesus' words become clearer. *"I no longer call you servants, because a servant does not know his master's business. Instead, I have called you friends, for everything that I learned from my Father I have made known to you"* (John 15:15); *"If you remain in me and my words remain in you, ask whatever you wish, and it will be given you"* (John 15:7).

I thank God for Anna Marie Dioso, a missionary based in Manila, Philippines, who has a God-given vision, burden, and compassion for exploited street children. Following a protracted time of prayer and fasting at a prayer mountain retreat, Anna Marie reported the following:

> It was a time set aside to pray exclusively for the red-light district in Manila which caters primarily to pedophiles (child molesters). One morning as I asked the Lord how to pray, He told me to speak out the Lordship of Jesus Christ over each night club by name. About six months after that, every bar closed and was boarded up by the Mayor of Manila. The President of the Philippines threatened to remove him from office due to the large number of complaints he was getting from the business district in that area. Hotels, money-changers, bar owners, restaurants, etc. were all losing their business—but so far, the bars remain closed. God is good!!!

THE PLIGHT OF CITIES

Jeremiah's close friendship with God was evidenced in his burdened and broken heart for the young people in his city. *"My eyes fail from weeping, I am in torment within, my heart is poured out on the ground because my people are destroyed, because children and infants faint in the streets of the city"* (Lamentations 2:11).

In the major cities of the United States the numbers of runaway youth have reached epidemic proportions. In Hollywood, California alone, there are between 20,000 and 22,000 of these young people. On any given summer night, between 1,000 and 4,000 are on the streets. Many of them have never told their parents where they are.

These disillusioned youth think that the big cities will give them excitement and freedom, which young people long for. They soon find out that when they have no money, cannot get a job, have nowhere to sleep, and have empty stomachs, Satan is quick to offer them a solution. They are desperate and destitute—longing for someone to care about them. They readily accept any offer of food, housing, and kindness.

Although drug pushers and pimps do the majority of the offering, there are also evangelical missions whose dedicated scouts are out there looking to help young people. One Saturday night, Jim and I paired off with two of our Youth With A Mission workers in Hollywood. At 2:30 a.m., the converted former prostitute I was with asked me if I wanted to go into a brothel with her to witness to some of her friends. I readily accepted. Jim and his partner waited in the car and interceded for us.

As we entered the room, my attractive African-American partner simply said, "Hi, this is my friend Joy" to three young prostitutes and their pimps who were seated on beds—the girls were taking a break. Since there were no chairs, we sat on the floor. I smiled warmly, said "Hi," and focused the conversation immediately on the Lord Jesus. Most of the people in the room were comfortable talking about Him. During the hour that I was there I learned that two of the girls and two of the pimps had formerly been exposed to the gospel, church, and Christians. The other pimp and his prostitute wore expressions as cold and lifeless as Egyptian sphinxes—and were as uncommunicative. The rest of the group entered into a lively dialogue with us. The former prostitute's radiant face was eloquent proof of the transforming work of Christ in her life.

Two of the prostitutes were bitter about experiences they'd had with Christians. I kept bringing the focus back to Jesus, our relationship with Him being the real issue. The girls readily agreed that there is no fault with Him. They chatted freely and respectfully with us. As we left, the head pimp, concerned for my safety, warned me that it could be pretty dangerous out on those streets at this time of night. I was touched by his genuine, warm concern.

As a way of life, I put the names or a description of the people to whom I witness on a list and pray regularly and fervently for their conversions. I added the names of those people to that long list, and prayed in faith for God to draw them to Himself. Three weeks later, one of the prostitutes was converted and went to live in one of the YWAM houses in downtown Hollywood. I met her again several months later when she had become a student at the Los Angeles YWAM Discipleship Training School. The transformation in her was so radical, I hardly recognized her. It was a very meaningful reunion.

Tragically, hundreds of runaway teenagers never make it out of their teens. They die, often through murder, drug over-dosing, and suicide.

The Los Angeles Police Department has a refrigerated morgue where hundreds of young bodies are covered and stacked on shelves with a label attached to a foot that reads "Unidentified." The bodies are kept in the morgue for three months before being cremated, just in case somebody comes to identify them. Mostly no one does.

WHAT ABOUT THE PARENTS?

The children aren't the only ones suffering. Multiplied thousands of parents in the world have children who have run away from home and have no idea where their children are. Thousands of parents have children who have mysteriously disappeared without any trace. I believe God is calling us to intercede for these parents in the following ways.

1. That God will use these parents' tragic circumstances to motivate them to turn to the Lord.

2. That parents will not be resentful toward God or their children, but rather will ask God to teach them what He wants them to learn through this time of suffering.

3. That parents will daily seek God diligently from His Word and expect Him to speak to them from it to meet their deepest needs.

4. That parents will see the situation as an opportunity to prove God's wonderful love, comfort, power, and faithfulness, and seek God for it and receive it by faith.

5.   That parents will believe that God will bring their children to submission and trust in Him, heal their wounded spirits and save their souls, and protect them and bring them home in the way and in the timing that will bring the greatest glory to His name.

Our loving heavenly Father knows what it's like to have a lost child. His only Son voluntarily became sin for us sinners. He had to be forsaken by the Father, that we may never be forsaken. The same loving heavenly Father who paid this ultimate price knows how to give the ultimate comfort.

Let us join forces in prayer with the parents that God will answer these requests and give them the supernatural peace that has no human explanation.

I have been involved in intercession with numbers of parents in this category, and we have seen mighty miracles. Some years ago, for example, the mother of a runaway teenager (whom she had not heard from for many months) and I cried out to God in faith that He would bring the boy back to God and to her. We prayed as though our lives depended upon that prayer, and took authority over the powers of darkness in relation to her boy. Exactly one week later to the very hour, he showed up at his mother's door. He was in terrible shape mentally, physically, emotionally, and spiritually—but he was there! Only God's power could have protected him in such a state and brought him the many hundreds of miles as he drove home. The son was slowly but surely restored. Today he has a heart for God and an evangelist's heart for the lost. Our loving, persistent, fervent prayers for parents and their children bring great results. Don't give up.

RADICAL CONVERTS, METHODS, AND RESULTS

It was 6:30 p.m. on a cold winter's night in downtown Los Angeles, two weeks before Christmas, 1992. It had been raining heavily all day, right up until that time. I stood in the long lines outside the Shrine Auditorium with thousands of others who were waiting for the doors to open for the event that was scheduled to start at 7:30 p.m. It was eight months after the Los Angeles riots.

What charged me with a deep inner excitement was that I had difficulty spotting any other Caucasians or anyone else over 35 years of age. I was thrilled to be in a distinct minority. I had longed and prayed much for this.

Seven thousand, mostly Latinos and African-Americans, showed up to see the performance. Hundreds from Victory Outreach, founded and directed by Sonny Argonzoni and his wife Julie, had blanketed the Los Angeles streets for weeks inviting gang members to come and see a two-hour drama presentation of life on the city streets and its implications— no holds barred.

Evangelist Mario Murillo had warned the audience ahead of time that this was not for the fearful or the squeamish. Scene after scene was acted out by former gang leaders and gang members, addicts, drug pushers, prostitutes, and pimps. They didn't have to be talented actors, although they were. They just needed to act out a rerun of their lives before having a life changing encounter with the living Christ. They did. It was shocking. It was dynamite ignited! The part that made the event so compelling was that it depicted stark reality.

One by one during the course of the show, a few of the actors dramatized how their clean cut commitment to the Lord Jesus Christ had resulted in a radical change. The other actors had chosen to reject the Lord's claims. There was no middle ground. No compromise. The implications of the gospel couldn't have been presented more clearly or more eloquently. When Mario Murillo invited the audience to make a similar choice, immediately the aisles were jammed with hundreds crowding forward to give their lives to Christ.

The man who headed up this outreach, Sonny Argonzoni, had himself been a desperate drug-addicted youth on the New York City streets until David Wilkerson had reached him with the gospel and Nicky Cruz had personally led him to the Lord in the '60s.

Today, Sonny Argonzoni has a powerfully anointed apostolic ministry to street people nationally and internationally. With God's enabling he has spawned churches in seven nations, including sixty-four cities in the United States. The pastors of these churches are all converts from the city streets. Two of them have earned the respect and trust of warring gang leaders in the San Fernando Valley in Los Angeles. Recently, several of the gang leaders have asked these men to help the gangs to live in peace instead of in the constant hate and fear that is accompanied by threats, fighting, beatings, shootings, and death.

This is certainly a breakthrough in answer to many years of fervent intercession. But there are still many gangs that are opposed to any form of reconciliation. The battle is far from won.

Of the 150,000 known gang members in the city of Los Angeles, 90 percent are arrested by age 18, and 60 percent are dead or in prison by age 20. What would happen if the members of the Church of Jesus Christ, His Body, stirred themselves up to take hold of God and persistently asked Him for the conversion of leading gang members in every city of the world, and believed Him to do it? What if they asked Him to bring forth apostles (like Sonny), prophets, evangelists (like Nicky Cruz), pastors (like the discipled converts in Victory Outreach), and teachers to reach the millions of desperately needy, disillusioned, frightened youth?

When we care enough about the pain behind the human need, regardless of the causes, we will get desperate with God in prayer.

One afternoon, Dr. Jerry Kirk, pastor of a thriving Presbyterian church in America, became desperate in prayer over the millions of sexually abused children in this country as a result of the rampant, ravaging, moral disease of pornography. He wept loudly, forcefully challenging God, asking Him what He was going to do about it.

Startled at his boldness in the light of Whom he challenged, Dr. Kirk drew a breath and waited. God's response was clear. "What are *you* going to do, Jerry?"

Jerry told God he would give the rest of his life, if necessary, in trying to stamp out pornography in the United States. God took him at his word. The National Coalition Against Pornography was conceived in Jerry's heart by the Holy Spirit, and has been and is being greatly used of God to stem the tide of this evil. Jerry Kirk had to be released from his pastoral ministry to accomplish this task.

What would happen if we became desperate enough to wrestle with God like Jacob, if necessary, until our hearts were broken over the pain of this generation of children and youth whom Satan has ravaged?

What would happen if we had a consuming burden in prayer to see a revolution of righteousness among this young generation, and made it a frequent request?

What would happen if we were prepared to engage in the spiritual warfare necessary to see young people set free from satanic chains that hold them prisoners?

What would happen if we were prepared to become part of the answers to our prayers and get involved in ministering to lost young people one-on-one?

What would happen if we were willing to invest our money in helping those who are already involved?

What would happen if we became desperate to see this generation of physically, verbally, and sexually abused, neglected, tormented, despairing, and suicidal youth made whole?

I know what would happen. God would pour out His Spirit worldwide, and we would see a breakthrough that would make headline news in the secular media. God did it before. It was called the Jesus movement. It's time for another breakthrough of even greater proportions. It's time to show the Church and the world that if Satan has the power to entice our youth to love and choose sin, God has far greater power to motivate them to love and choose righteousness. It's called revival. It's needed for our children's survival!

SUGGESTED PRAYER

Loving Heavenly Father,

I take comfort and encouragement from knowing that because of Your loving concern for the harassed and hurting youth and children of the world, You have plans to deliver and heal them.

Fill my heart with Your love for them and use me in whichever way You choose, in the outworking of those plans and the fulfillment of their destinies.

I want to respond to Your call through Jeremiah, whose heart reflected Yours. "Arise, cry out in the night, as the watches of the night begin; pour out your heart like water in the presence of the Lord. Lift up your hands to him for the lives of your children, who faint from hunger at the head of every street" (Lamentations 2:19). Thank You that You will work in me and through me to answer this prayer.

In Jesus' all-powerful name, Amen.

7

How Intercession Works

New Zealand was where I was born and raised. As a result of Loren Cunningham's extended visit to our home in 1967, I received invitations during 1968–69 from seven nations to come and teach the Word of God. In January 1970, at the clear call of God and with my dear husband's full approval and support, I started my journey.

For the month of February, I taught at the YWAM School of Evangelism in Switzerland on the character and ways of God. One time I was seeking God as to which aspect of these subjects I was to teach for a morning class. Suddenly thoughts darted into my mind like arrows from a well-aimed bow and lodged there. They came as questions: What do I do that releases the power of God in prayer for others? What are the simple steps of obedience that produce the thrilling, fulfilling ministry of intercession? I was very aware that what I had been teaching had come from many years of deep personal experience based upon the Word of God.

My mind quickly returned to New Zealand—to the times I had interceded for the nations of the world alone. To the two years of praying for the nations every Thursday afternoon with my dear prayer partner Shelagh McAlpine before she returned to England to live. To the years following, when my close friends Hazel Elliott and Dorothy Leonard became my prayer partners for the same purpose.

The questions persisted—demanding answers. "Well, what do you do that makes it all happen?" The unity in the Spirit, the times of remarkable revelation, the feeling of having accomplished more for the extension of God's kingdom than in any other Christian activity in which I've been engaged. I quickly jotted down what I do in childlike obedience to the promptings of the Holy Spirit, remembering carefully the order.

The result: ten simple steps. On Friday morning in that classroom, God directed me to share those steps for the first time. I could never have dreamed that God in His sovereignty would take them, more than any other part of my teaching on intercession, and have them used in many parts of the world. The steps have been translated into many languages and have been published in numerous books and periodicals. The promotion has been strictly God's. I've always been amazed by it.

There are many ways to have vital times of intercession. I am not saying this is the only way. I'm simply sharing some guidelines that have been proven by many to help people hear God's voice and pray His thoughts back to Him on behalf of others. Here they are:

PRINCIPLES FOR EFFECTIVE INTERCESSION

1. Praise God for who He is. God's power is especially released through worshipful song.

"*As they began to sing and praise, the* Lord *set ambushes against [the enemy], and they were defeated*" (2 Chronicles 20:22).

Praise God for the privilege of engaging in the same wonderful ministry as the Lord Jesus, as you cooperate with Him in prayer relating to the affairs of men. "*...he always lives to intercede for them*" (Hebrews 7:25b).

2. Make sure your heart is clean before God by giving the Holy Spirit time to convict should you have any unconfessed sin.

"*If I had cherished sin in my heart, the* LORD *would not have listened*" (Psalm 66:18).

"*Search me, O God, and know my heart; test me and know my anxious thoughts. See if there is any offensive way in me, and lead me in the way everlasting*" (Psalm 139:23–24).

We can also be encouraged by God's promise that if we draw near to Him, He will draw near to us—just as we are. As we seek His face, not His hand, worshiping and waiting on Him, He will do His purifying work in us.

Check carefully in relation to the sin of resentment to anyone, and make sure you've forgiven those who've wronged you.

Notice the link between forgiveness and effective prayer in God's Word. Both during Jesus' instruction to His disciples on how to pray in what is commonly known as the Lord's Prayer and immediately following it, Jesus emphasizes the need to release forgiveness to those who have wronged us.

"*And when you stand praying, if you hold anything against anyone, forgive him, so that your Father in heaven may forgive you your sins*" (Mark 11:25).

Now notice the link between forgiveness and faith when we pray: "*…whatever you ask for in prayer, believe that you have received it, and it will be yours*" (Mark 11:24).

Another powerful reminder of this truth is in Luke 17:3–5: "*So watch yourselves. If your brother sins, rebuke him, and if he repents, forgive him. If he sins against you seven times in a day, and seven times comes back to you and says, 'I repent,' forgive him. The apostles said to the* LORD, '*Increase our faith!*'" [emphasis added].

The disciples knew that to live this teaching would require an enlargement of faith, because forgiveness is not easy when one has been repeatedly wronged and hurt. Jesus' answer assured them that increased faith for greater effectiveness in prayer was not only necessary, but also possible (verse 6).

Job had to forgive his friends for their wrong judging of him before he could pray effectively for them (Job 42:10). "*…faith [expresses] itself through love*" (Galatians 5:6). Part of true love is forgiving those who have wronged us.

3. Acknowledge that you can't really pray effectively without the Holy Spirit's enabling.

"...*the Spirit helps us in our weakness. We do not know what we ought to pray for*" (Romans 8:26b).

Ask God to utterly control you by His Spirit, receive by faith that He does, and thank Him. "...*be filled with the Spirit*" (Ephesians 5:18b).

It is only as the Holy Spirit is given access to pray through our cleansed, yielded, spirit-controlled lives that we will become and remain effective intercessors. Power in prayer is released through purity.

It is entirely possible to experience the voice of the Holy Spirit in direction, and have little or no Spirit-charged energy to make the prayer effective. On one occasion I had gone to prayer over someone who was in great spiritual need. I knew God had burdened my heart, and I was praying the right words. But I felt as though they were not getting farther than the ceiling. I stopped and inquired, "God, why isn't there power behind these words? They're falling flat and not reaching your throne. Is there a blockage due to undealt-with sin in my life?"

The conviction of sin came swiftly and with piercing clarity. The Holy Spirit revealed that I had loved speeding all my life and had indulged in it whenever I could—regardless of the fact that to do so I had to break the law.

Many times I had confessed the sin of breaking the law in this way, but now the Holy Spirit was showing me that this was not repentance. Repentance is being sorry enough about the sin to quit. It is having a change of mind, heart, and life toward the sin. It is having the fear of God toward that sin, which is to hate it (Proverbs 8:13).

I obviously loved the sin of driving too fast, that's why I chose to do it all too frequently.

That day I deeply repented before God and asked Him to put the fear of God upon me in relation to this aspect of breaking the law. I received by faith that He would do just that. He did. Believe me, it was revolutionary. I went back to pray for the needy person. This time I felt divine energy behind my intercession. Purity and power are synonymous with God.

While writing this book, I came across a transcript of a message on intercession I had given many years before. In it was the above illustration. I knew when I read it that God was reminding me of this lesson. Over the years, I had become less sensitive than I should be about the speed limit. Fresh repentance was the remedy.

"Who may ascend the hill of the Lord? *Who may stand in his holy place? He who has clean hands and a pure heart, ...He will receive blessing from the* Lord*"* (Psalm 24:3–5a).

4. Deal aggressively with the enemy. Come against him in the all-powerful name of the Lord Jesus Christ and with the sword of the Spirit—the Word of God.

"Submit yourselves, then, to God. Resist the devil, and he will flee from you" (James 4:7).

5. Die to your own imaginations, desires and burdens for what you feel you should pray.

The need for this act of the will is clearly stated as follows: *"...lean not on your own understanding"* (Proverbs 3:5b); *"He who trusts in his own mind is a fool"* (Proverbs 28:26a RSV); *"For my thoughts are not your thoughts"* (Isaiah 55:8a).

6. Praise God now in faith for the remarkable prayer time you're going to have.

He's a remarkable God and will do something consistent with His character.

7. Wait before God in silent expectancy, listening for His direction.

"But my people would not listen to me; Israel would not submit to me. So I gave them over to their stubborn hearts to follow their own devices. If my people would but listen to me, if Israel would follow my ways" (Psalm 81:11–13); *"For God alone my soul waits in silence, for my hope is from him"* (Psalm 62:5 RSV); *"But as for me, I will look to the* Lord, *I will wait for the God of my salvation; my God will hear me"* (Micah 7:7 RSV).

8. In obedience and faith, take action on what God brings to your mind, believing.

"My sheep listen to my voice...and they follow me" (John 10:27).

Keep asking God for direction, expecting Him to give it to you. He will. *"I will instruct you and teach you in the way you should go; I will counsel you and watch over you"* (Psalm 32:8).

Make sure you don't move on to the next subject until you've given God time to discharge all He wants to say to you regarding the present focus, especially when praying in a group. It's not necessary for everyone in the group to receive directional revelation. But it is necessary for all to cooperate with those who do, providing the Holy Spirit witnesses in each heart that the directions are coming from Him. Guard against any one person dominating the prayers.

9. If possible, have your Bible with you should God want to give you direction or confirmation through His Word.

"Your word is a lamp to my feet and a light for my path" (Psalm 119:105).

10. When God ceases to bring things to your mind for which to pray, finish by praising and thanking Him for what He has done, reminding yourself that "...from him and through him and to him are all things. To him be the glory forever! Amen" (Romans 11:36).

The following remarkable and far-reaching results from applying these biblical principles were recounted to me by an associate pastor from a church in Pennsylvania.

During the winter of 1981 and the spring of 1982, I had been calling out to the Lord for an outpouring of His Spirit in this area. He led me to open a leadership prayer breakfast in a local restaurant, and impressed upon me the need for intercessory prayer. A book-marker containing your Principles for Effective Intercession was given to me by one of the women in our church. We began to implement these every Thursday morning for two hours as pastors and lay leaders came together to pray.

The group grew from four, to about 30, and over a two year period things began to happen. Some of which were:

- two new churches were established in our state
- missionaries were sent to Scotland, England, Nepal, India, Guatemala, Mexico, and Russia
- a night club which had exotic dancers was closed down
- there was an economic recovery in the local steel industry
- prostitutes came to Christ
- x-rated theaters were closed
- a well known Christian leader's book was circulated among the businessmen in three communities
- the represented churches experienced growth both in number and in spirit.

[The pastor went on to say:]

We understand that it is God who works in us both to will and to do His pleasure. I must say that your guidelines for intercession were the channel which brought us into a position to receive the Lord's blessings.

SUGGESTED PRAYER

Dear God,

I understand that if I want the maximum effectiveness to result from my times of intercession, I may well have to be more prepared. Thank You that You will teach me and enable me.

In Jesus' name, Amen.

8

How Big Is Your Vision?

*I*f your vision is not world vision, it's too small. *"He has...set eternity in the hearts of men"* (Ecclesiastes 3:11b).

The Body of Christ internationally has many great visionaries, but relatively few world visionaries. How big is your vision for all the world to be reached with the gospel, and disciples made for Christ? The answer is simple and direct: to the measure in which your daily lifestyle contributes to its accomplishment.

The Bible has hundreds of references to the nations, and where God places great emphasis, so should we.

We can gather reams of statistics about the needs in the world today or about nations being reached with the gospel, yet never become personally involved. A newspaper reporter could do the same. Or, we may be involved in reaching the lost and seeing them discipled in our own nation, denomination, missionary society, church, city, neighborhood, friends, or family, yet not have world vision. Vision determines our priorities, and our priorities determine our destinies.

We need to frequently pray the prayer of Jabez, *"Oh, that you would bless me and enlarge my territory! Let your hand be with me"* (1 Chronicles 4:10b). "Enlarge my territory" simply means enlarge my vision; increase my sphere of influence and ability through the power of the Holy Spirit to make You known on this earth. God will always answer that prayer. *"And God granted his request"* (1 Chronicles 4:10d).

Do we really understand that every time we ask God to bless us, it is so that the nations may be more effectively reached with the gospel and disciples made for the Lord Jesus Christ? That's no small purpose for being blessed. *"May God be gracious to us and bless us and make his face shine upon us, that your ways may be known on earth, your salvation among all nations"* (Psalm 67:1–2). That's no small vision. It involves world vision.

Before we look at what it means to be involved, let's look at God's undisputable, unimpeachable authority over the nations. *"Let the heavens rejoice, let the earth be glad; let them say among the nations, 'The LORD reigns!'"* (1 Chronicles 16:31).

The news I hear on television or the radio, or read in the newspaper can be startling, devastating, shocking, and terrifying, but I can say, "Hallelujah, the Lord is the ruling, reigning monarch of the universe!" He's not only the Commander-in-Chief. He's actively involved. *"He makes nations great, and destroys them; he enlarges nations, and disperses them"* (Job 12:23). This is no big deal when we consider His unparalleled greatness. The nations shrink down in size to their true proportions in the light of His magnitude.

We frequently talk about large, powerful nations, but God's perspective of them is vastly different from ours. He thinks of them in relation to Himself. *"Surely the nations are like a drop in a bucket; they are regarded as dust on the scales; ...Before him all the nations are as nothing; they are regarded by him as worthless and less than nothing"* (Isaiah 40:15a, 17).

In light of that peek through God's eyes, what impresses us as powerful becomes ludicrous! God is the only being who is really big. Everything and everyone are comparatively microscopic. I'm totally impressed with Him! When this concept grips us, our "motivation battery" is charged, and our "faith juices" are stimulated to believe that our involvement with the nations is going to produce results.

WORLD VISION REQUIRES ACTION IN THREE AREAS OF OUR LIVES

1. Intercession

We are to intercede not for some nations, or for many nations, but for all the nations. God doesn't leave us with any doubt about our particular responsibility in that regard. Jesus stood in the temple and made public reference to the word of the Lord through the prophet Isaiah: "...*my house will be called a house of prayer for all nations*" (Isaiah 56:7b).

God instructs us to ask Him to radically change the course of the history of the nations and promises equally radical results when we do. "*Ask of me, and I will make the nations your inheritance, the ends of the earth your possession. You will rule them with an iron scepter; you will dash them to pieces like pottery*" (Psalm 2:8–9).

Obligation

In fact, praying for the nations is of such importance to God that He gives it priority, even before praying for national and international leaders. Paul admonishes, "*I urge, then, first of all, that requests, prayers, intercession and thanksgiving be made for everyone*" (1 Timothy 2:1). The only way we can do that is to have a prayer plan that includes peoples of every nation in the world.

Is your church a house of prayer for *all* the nations? Does it have a systematic plan of involving the congregation in praying for the 218 countries of the world? Is your home a house of prayer for *all* the nations?

Suggested Intercession Methods

One method of interceding for the nations is to follow the steps outlined in chapter 7, and ask God to impress upon your mind the country for which He wants you to pray.

Another method is to systematically and regularly pray through the list of countries at the back of this book, targeting one or several per day or week, or however God directs you individually. I have used both methods effectively for many years.

Another effective method of discharging these responsibilities is to use YWAM's international prayer diary that lists a different nation or people group for daily prayer. Or use Every Home for Christ Crusade's prayer plan that incorporates a world map with a listing of every country.

The main thing is to realize that we are responsible to be obedient to God's clear mandate to pray for all nations. Ask God which method or methods He wants you to use and keep to them with consistency. Of course there's a price time-wise for this involvement, but where there's a will there's a way. We make time for what we really want to do. Our making time for God's priorities is really the issue.

It is of enormous benefit to ask God to give you a prayer partner or partners, and then intercede with them on a regular basis for the nations, as directed by the Holy Spirit. These times can become some of the most exhilarating, far-reaching, interesting prayer meetings in which we can be involved.

When I lived in New Zealand, my prayer partners, Dorothy Leonard and Hazel Elliott and I were waiting on God for the Holy Spirit's direction. We had gathered in my home to pray for the nations. In time, Africa clearly became the focus.

It was at the time of the uprising of the Cimbas in the Congo during the 1960s. Gradually but pointedly, God orchestrated our prayers to tune in on one particular woman missionary belonging to the Worldwide Evangelization Crusade (WEC). She had been reported missing from her mission's base for some time and was presumed dead. Other WEC missionaries had been murdered by the Cimbas. No hope was given for the woman's life.

It was a real step of faith just to speak her name, let alone continue in prayer for her. However, direction to pray for her life to be spared and for her protection came to us from specific Scriptures quickened by the Holy Spirit as we continued to diligently seek God. This removed presumption, speculation, or a passive resignation to the hopelessness of the reports. We also engaged in spiritual warfare against the powers of darkness on the woman's behalf.

We simply believed that having applied the principles outlined in chapter 7 of this book, God was the explanation of the impressions we were receiving. We believed God for the woman's life to be spared, and we gave Him praise. Later God wonderfully used my evening reading in the little devotional book of Scriptures called *The Daily Light* to confirm that the Holy Spirit had directed us, and had heard and answered our prayers.

The first Scripture was "...*God has revealed it to us by his Spirit*" (1 Corinthians 2:10a), and the second was "...*The knowledge of the secrets of the kingdom of heaven has been given to you...*" (Matthew 13:11).

In faith I told my family that evening that my prayer partners and I believed that the missionary was alive and asked them to say nothing to anyone but to quietly wait with us for God to reverse the announcements in His perfect time. They cooperated and were intrigued, to say the least.

The next day the secular press announced the woman missionary's death. The World Evangelization Crusade headquarters in Auckland, New Zealand, was notified of her death. The woman's father in New Zealand was officially notified of her death. Weeks later, the news came through to New Zealand from the Congo that the lady missionary, presumed dead, was very much alive and well. The newspaper headlines read, "Missionary, as one brought back from the dead." The woman had been captured by the Cimbas but was later rescued by three nuns who hid her and cared for her, and subsequently took her back to the other missionaries. The woman's rescue occurred on the very day we were praying for her miraculous deliverance.

Satan and demonic powers are aware of the effectiveness of this kind of prayer meeting, so be prepared for their efforts to thwart you. Take aggressive action against them in the name of the Lord Jesus Christ, using the Word of God as a sword (for example, James 4:7). Make a commitment to follow through, regardless of their tactics. In time they'll get the message that you refuse to be distracted.

This concept of praying regularly for the nations may be new to many. Perhaps you could suggest to your pastor or the leader of your mission or prayer group that you have a meeting at least once a month to intercede for the nations. Praying together in small groups is ideal.

Ways to Stimulate Intercession

The following are some practical ideas for stimulating intercession for the nations in your home.

    a. Feed information into your home on world missions through missionary societies' magazines and books. What kind of magazines in your home are the most accessible to your family? The following publications give vital, current information related to world evangelization:

    ❧ Youth With A Mission's quarterly publication, *World Christian News*, Youth With A Mission, P.O. Box 26479, Colorado Springs, CO 80936-6479.

    ❧ The U.S. Center for World Missions' bulletin, *Mission Frontiers*, 1605 Elizabeth Street, Pasadena, CA 91104. The bulletin is published every other month.

    b. Open your home in hospitality to God's servants who are involved in world missions.

    c. At every opportunity, share with your family vital stories you've read and heard of where the unevangelized are being reached with the gospel. This inspires prayer involvement.

    d. Teach your family (the younger you start them the better) to pray individually during family worship time for the needs among nations to which you've exposed them. Tell them they can expect to hear God's voice, and let the Holy Spirit direct their prayers. Encourage them from the Bible with God's promises: "*...the sheep listen to his voice...and his sheep follow him because they know his voice*" (John 10:3b–4b); "*I will instruct you and teach you in the way you should go; I will counsel you and watch over you*" (Psalm 32:8).

e. Pray regularly that God will involve your whole family in world evangelism, and by so doing ruin them for the ordinary. By God's grace, Jim and I consistently followed through with this. Our son and daughter, along with us, have been in full-time missionary work since 1971.

f. Give hospitality to and share God's love with foreign students. Pray for their salvation, and wisely witness to them.

2. Our Response to the Great Commission

The second area of our life in which action is required with regard to world vision is our response to the Great Commission.

We can have world vision only to the degree we have taken the following mandates seriously:

"Therefore go and make disciples of all nations, baptizing them in the name of the Father and of the Son and of the Holy Spirit, and teaching them to obey everything I have commanded you. And surely I am with you always, to the very end of the age" (Matthew 28:19–20).

"Declare his glory among the nations, his marvelous deeds among all peoples" (1 Chronicles 16:24).

To avoid hypocrisy, we must be willing to become part of the answers to our prayers for the nations. The Great Commission is directed to every Christian. It has no age limit, requires no educational status, and places no stipulations regarding health or finances. None of us can dodge its implications. The command is to "Go." That requires a change of location, whether for a short, or for a long duration. *We'll never know or experience God's ultimate plan for our lives until we've responded to this clear call from the mouth of the Lord Jesus.*

What have we done to prepare ourselves to be sent? We may have said we were willing to be sent by God anywhere, anytime. But how much listening time have we given Him, seeking His face for any directional change He may want to give us? God's directions come to a willing, available, listening, seeking heart. A heart that says to Him, "Because you said 'go into all the world,' you'll need to give me clear direction and much grace if you should choose to tell me to stay."

Listen to the heart cry of God, because so few give God quality listening time. *"But my people would not listen to me; Israel would not submit to me. So I gave them over to their stubborn hearts to follow their own devices. If my people would but listen to me, if Israel would follow my ways"* (Psalm 81:11–13).

We're never too old, and it's never too late. God is still looking for Calebs who will *"follow the* Lord *[their] God wholeheartedly"* (Joshua 14:8b). Three students at one of YWAM's special missions training schools in Kona, Hawaii, for 35-year-olds and older, were in their 80s. These three octogenarians were among the keenest in their class. Their story was "Better late than never."

Another illustration comes from our New Zealand friends, Keith and Bell Liddle, who responded to the call of God to do missionary work in Indonesia when Keith was 65, and his wife Bell was 62.

The Liddles had already planned their retirement years. They had made building plans for their new home in a beautiful, scenic location, but they left it all for the mission field. Their testimony, after ten years, was that those missionary years had been the best times of their lives in every way. And they had lived full and productive lives in active Christian service before their response to overseas missions.

I was also intrigued to meet a unique married couple in the United States who weren't converted until their 60s. Prior to their conversion, they had developed a corporation that dealt in various fields of ecology. Tom was a scientist; Joan, the business manager. The couple later sold their very successful business and sailed around the world in a forty-eight-foot sailing vessel that Joan had built largely with her own hands. In the process she wore out her wedding ring and had to have it replaced!

This couple had been involved in scientology and other meditative religious groups. Later they moved to South

Carolina, where they attended a small Baptist church and were converted. During the time that they attended a Christian training program, they sought God diligently for the future course of their lives. God directed them to fast, with the understanding that at the end of twelve days they would know where He would send them as missionaries. Right on schedule, as promised, He spoke to them, telling them individually that they were to go to Togoland. They didn't even know where it was.

Tom was 69 years of age and Joan was 64 when the couple went to Togo and attended a language school. Eight years later, in 1993, they had built and established over sixty churches. Tom was 77 and Joan was 72. They operated by training nationals and generally overseeing the work in Togo, spending about half their time there and half in America. A truly remarkable Caleb couple of the first order!

As Tom and Joan demonstrate, the years normally allotted to retirement can become the most thrilling, rewarding, and fulfilling years of a lifetime.

The Bible promises that senior citizens can be among the most fruitful, and experience the greatest blessings from God. *The righteous will flourish like a palm tree, they will grow like a cedar of Lebanon; planted in the house of the* Lord, *they will flourish in the courts of our God. They will still bear fruit in old age, they will stay fresh and green, proclaiming, 'The* Lord *is upright; he is my Rock, and there is no wickedness in him'"* (Psalm 92:12–15).

We can choose the boredom of retirement or the adventure of "refirement." I've made my choice.

3. Giving Financially

The third area of action is financial giving. Jesus said, *"For where your treasure is, there your heart will be also"* (Matthew 6:21).

If we want to have vision for the world to be evangelized, we need to be giving regularly from our resources for its accomplishment. The Bible says our treasure will be where our heart is. God's heart beats with a passion for the nations to be reached with the gospel. How much of our offerings (over and above our tithes) are directed to world evangelization in general? And how much of our giving is specifically directed towards evangelizing the unreached?

SUGGESTED PRAYER

Praise You, Lord, for enlarging my vision. Thank You for stretching me, challenging me, and inspiring me to believe that You have a plan to use me in new ways for world evangelization.

I am a candidate for change. Fulfill all Your eternal purposes in my life, especially as they relate to the nations of the world.

I will not make suggestions or excuses or dictate the terms. Nor will I limit You in any way through unbelief. You have blessed me so that Your ways may be known on earth, and Your salvation among all nations.

Show me now, before I stand before You to give an account of the stewardship of my life, what You require of me before You can say, "Well done, good and faithful servant." Thank You that You will, because You are faithful.

In Jesus' name, Amen.

9

Prayer Strategies for Changing Nations

*E*very one of us has the opportunity to affect the course of history in our lifetime. Few realize this and take the opportunity. Every time an intercessor prays effectively for a nation, God's hand is moved. When this happens, the greatest forces of power in the universe are mobilized, and history is made. Intercessors praying regularly and effectively for the nations become some of the greatest history shapers of all time.

As we pray for the nations of the world, it is important to understand that our main focus needs to be on the Body of Christ in those nations. God has shaped history around His people, and He expects us—not governments—to shape the history of the nations (2 Chronicles 7:14).

We will understand the responsibility of God's people, the Church, in relation to the nations of the world now, only when we understand the responsibility and privilege for which God is preparing the Church in the future. God is preparing His Church to share with Him, as His Bride, His sovereign power and authority over His eternal kingdom. *"To him who overcomes and does my will to the end, I will give authority over the nations"* (Revelation 2:26); *"Then the sovereignty, power and greatness of the kingdoms under the whole* heaven will be handed over to the saints, the people of the Most High. His kingdom will be an everlasting kingdom, and all rulers will worship and obey him" (Daniel 7:27).

Paul had this revelation when He wrote to the Corinthians: "*Do you not know that the saints will judge the world? ...Do you not know that we will judge angels?*" (1 Corinthians 6:2–3a). When he wrote to the Ephesians, Paul was trying to get them to see the big picture: "*I pray that your hearts will be flooded with light so that you can see something of the future he has called you to share*" (Ephesians 1:18 TLB).

As we cooperate with God in shaping the history of the nations, God reshapes us. We can expect to be purified and changed. God is preparing His Church to "*...present her to himself as a radiant church, without stain or wrinkle or any other blemish, but holy and blameless. ...Christ loved the Church and gave himself up for her to make her holy*" (Ephesians 5:27, 25b–26a).

We need to check our lives with each point we pray to make sure we're living what we're praying. If we're not, then repentance will qualify us to become effective. It's the effectual fervent prayer of a righteous person that prevails (James 5:16).

The following outline will help us to pray effectively.

1.   Thank and praise God for who He is and for the privilege of cooperating with Him in this exciting ministry. Then thank Him for what He's already done in the nations to which He has directed us.

"*...with thanksgiving, present your requests to God*" (Philippians 4:6).

2.   Pray for an unprecedented outpouring of the Holy Spirit in revival power to come upon God's people.

The psalmist prayed; "*Will you not revive us again, that your people may rejoice in you?*" (Psalm 85:6). The way I interpret that prayer and use it is like this: "Come and do something with us that only You can do that will powerfully motivate us to deeply repent of all idolatry—everything that keeps us from making You our supreme longing, our first love, and our greatest purpose for living."

Isaiah gives us one of the most powerful prayers for revival that we can pray: *"Oh, that you would rend the heavens and come down, that the mountains would tremble before you! As when fire sets twigs ablaze and causes water to boil, come down to make your name known to your enemies and cause the nations to quake before you! For when you did awesome things that we did not expect, you came down, and the mountains trembled before you* (Isaiah 64:1–3).

"Awesome things that we did not expect" is a perfect definition of true revival, because the unpredictable and the unusual are characteristics of great spiritual awakenings.

Revival is God greatly stirring, shaking, and changing His people from apathy, selfishness and self-promotion to a repentant, humble, fervently praying, and praising people. People with a passion only for God and His glory, and a far greater burden for the lost. A spiritual awakening among the lost follows, resulting in a great harvest of souls coming into the kingdom of God.

The hallmarks of genuine revival are currently taking place in an Assemblies of God church in Pensacola, Florida. From a recent report, over 86,000 people have responded to the anointed preaching of the gospel, either for salvation or for repentance from backsliding, during the past twenty-two months. An equal emphasis on God's holiness and God's love characterizes the preaching to the multitudes of believers and the unconverted who continue to pour into the services. A mature pastor friend who visited this revival wrote me and said, "The worship was electric, and far beyond anything I had ever seen." He continued to say, "The worship, which lasts for hours, comes to a high peak and then when you think it couldn't go any higher, it does."

There has been an awesome sense of God's manifest presence and power in the meetings, resulting in many thousands of changed lives, including pastors and lay people. This outpouring of God's Spirit was preceded by two years of desperate, focused community prayer for revival. The revival continues four nights of every week. People start arriving from between 8 am to 10 am to make sure they have a seat for an evening service. Many are fervently praying for this divine visitation to continue and to spread like prairie fire.

We need to pray for God to stir His people in each nation to see the vision for revival, to be aware of the desperate need for it, and to know that it has no substitute. We need to pray that God's people will intercede persistently for revival, to be prepared for it, and be ready to be used in it.

We need to believe God's promises to send worldwide revival as we persist in prayer. Here is just one of many promises listed in chapter 18: "*For as the soil makes the sprout come up and a garden causes seeds to grow, so the Sovereign* LORD *will make righteousness and praise spring up before all nations*" (Isaiah 61:11).

3. Pray for God to unite the Body of Christ.

According to the prayer of Jesus in John 17:23, unity is the greatest factor to influence the lost to commit their lives to Christ: "*I in them and you in me. May they be brought to complete unity to let the world know that you sent me and have loved them even as you have loved me.*"

Pray for God to convict His people of the pride and prejudice that separates them, and that the realization will come that without unity His people will suffer defeat. "*Every kingdom divided against itself will be ruined, and every city or household divided against itself will not stand*" (Matthew 12:25b).

Pray for God to release a spirit of humility that will bring the realization of our desperate need for one another.

God's present, great emphasis on reconciliation and unity is the purpose for the historic things that are taking place around the world through the International Reconciliation Coalition.

God is requiring Christian leaders worldwide to take the lead in humbling themselves in acts of identificational repentance, confessing the sins of our forefathers where divisions have originated, and asking for forgiveness.

On reconciliation walks, believers are apologizing to two million Muslims and Jews over the next three years, for the way the Crusaders greatly distorted the character of God to these people 900 years ago, and asking for the Muslims' and Jews' forgiveness. The walks are taking place along the routes that the Crusaders took.

The Holy Spirit is breaking down centuries old barriers that have divided many people groups relationally:

- Gentiles and Jews
- Arabs and Jews
- Messianic Jews and Gentile believers
- Catholics and protestants
- Ethnic groups
- Males and females
- The older and younger generations
- The host people of a land and those who unjustly came and took it over from them
- Muslims and Christians
- Muslims, Jews, and Christians

Wherever there are divisions in the Body of Christ, reconciliation and the biblical standards of unity (John 17:21, 23) must take place before the glory of God is manifest on God's people as promised in John 17:22.

Pursuing this depth of unity should be given a priority place in all our relationships, and in private and public intercession.

Pray that the Body of Christ will encourage, support, and intercede for one another, be willing to work together, and above all learn from each other.

4. We need to humble ourselves before God and acknowledge that the Body of Christ in our nation deserves judgment because of idolatry, apathy, disobedience to revealed truth, and the spirit of the world that pervades it.

We identify with the sins of the people of God like Nehemiah and substitute the name of our nation for Israel.

"Let your ear be attentive and your eyes open to hear the prayer your servant is praying before you day and night for your servants, the people of Israel. I confess the sins we Israelites, including myself and my father's house, have committed against

you. We have acted very wickedly toward you. We have not obeyed the commands, decrees and laws you gave your servant Moses" (Nehemiah 1:6–7).

Cry to God for mercy: *"O Lord...In this time of our deep need, begin again to help us, as you did in years gone by. Show us your power to save us. In your wrath, remember mercy"* (Habakkuk 3:2 TLB).

In God's time, as we persist and prevail in prayer, results are assured. Be encouraged from Habakkuk 3:3–6; *God came manifesting His holiness, glory, majesty, judgment, and awesome power.*

5. Pray for leaders.

First, we pray for God to raise up spiritual leaders from the five ministries mentioned in Ephesians 4:11, and pray that they will be men and women of integrity who will fear the Lord and operate according to the character and ways of God. We pray that leaders will be given national and international vision related to the extension of God's kingdom (Proverbs 29:18).

Then we pray for present national leadership (1 Timothy 2:1–2), remembering that *"the authorities that exist have been established by God"* (Romans 13:1b). We must accept God's sovereign purpose in having placed leaders in authority, and pray for them with a loving heart, believing, as we do, that God is working. *"The only thing that counts is faith expressing itself through love"* (Galatians 5:6b).

I once heard at a conference a Christian speech writer for external affairs from a certain nation report the following encouraging story. A member of Parliament was going to another city and was planning on visiting pornography shops and strip bars. On the morning before he left, he found three letters in the mail from people who said they were praying regularly for him. He told a colleague that because of the effect those letters had on him, he decided not to be unfaithful to his wife by going to those shops and bars.

It is important also to pray that God will promote righteous leaders and put them in positions of authority and influence in the Church, the government, the judicial system, the educational system, business and commerce, the medical profession, the media, sports, the arts, and entertainment. *"When a country is rebellious, it has many rulers, but a man of understanding and knowledge maintains order"* (Proverbs 28:2).

6. **Pray that the Word of God will be given its rightful place as the basis for the formation of just laws, and as the standard for moral values and behavior.**

Cry out to God; *"It is time for you to act, O LORD; your law is being broken"* (Psalm 119:126). Pray that the spiritual heads of homes will take their place of responsibility by teaching their children from the Bible and having family worship together. Pray that the Bible will be translated, published, and distributed in the language of every people group, and that it will be read daily, understood, believed, and obeyed (Psalm 119:130).

7. **Pray that God will stir His people to see that obedience is the key to the Christian life.**

Pray that God's priorities will become our daily priorities by:

a. Living a life of worship that becomes the basis of everything we do; otherwise idolatry is inevitable (Matthew 4:10).

b. Spending time alone with God

* in intercession for others.

* in getting to know God by studying His character and ways from His Word.

* in waiting on God for His directions. *"But my people would not listen to me; Israel would not submit to me. So I gave them over to their stubborn hearts to follow their own devices"* (Psalm 81:11–12).

c. Having a burdened heart for the lost that will motivate us to witness, and expecting to lead people to the Lord Jesus. *" 'Come, follow me,' "* Jesus said, *" 'and I will make you fishers of men' "* (Matthew 4:19). If we're not witnessing when the Holy Spirit prompts us, we're not following Jesus.

d. Seeing the need to fulfill the conditions of being empowered by the Holy Spirit, *"Do not get drunk on wine, which leads to debauchery. Instead, be filled with the Spirit"* (Ephesians 5:18).

Pray that God will reveal that the above priorities are possible only as God's commands are obeyed, and that all our service is powerless and ineffective without His enduement.

8. Pray for the fear of the Lord to permeate all believers, because the fear of the Lord is the beginning of wisdom and knowledge, and it means to hate evil (Proverbs 8:13).

Pray for a passion for holiness to grip the hearts of God's people as it did with the early Church. They walked in the fear of the Lord. *"...let us purify ourselves from everything that contaminates body and spirit, perfecting holiness out of reverence for God"* (2 Corinthians 7:1b). Purity of life is essential for sustained power, which operates when applied to human need.

9. Pray for the children and youth. (See chapter 6.)
   a. That they'll be given a chance to be born, hear the gospel, and respond in great numbers.
   b. That God will raise up children and youth ministries in increasing numbers.
   c. That the young will be taught about the character and ways of God.
   d. That God will bring revival among them.
   e. That deliverance and healing will come to the many abused and neglected children.
   f. That God will sovereignly reveal Himself to young people, and that they'll know He loves them and cares about their pain.

10. Pray for God to thrust forth laborers into the whitened harvest fields of the world (Matthew 9:38), from every nation and into each nation (Matthew 28:19–20).

Prayer is still the greatest recruiting force for the fulfillment of the Great Commission. Pray that the realization will come to every believer that the mandate to "go to the nations" has been given without exception. Therefore, everyone should prepare to go, expect to be sent, desire to go, and need God's grace to stay at home should God clearly direct.

11. Ask God to stir the spiritual leaders to teach people from the Bible about their need to be involved with the poor and needy.

A number of Scriptures command our involvement with hurting people and warn us of God's judgment if we disobey. One warning is, *"If a man shuts his ears to the cry of the poor, he too will cry out and not be answered"* (Proverbs 21:13). Paul exhorts us to remember to pray for believers who are mistreated and imprisoned for their faith (Hebrews 13:3).

12. Pray for a great spiritual awakening to come upon the unconverted, motivating them to seek God.

Pray for unrighteous leaders in positions of authority and influence to be saved. Then pray for the most unlikely people to be converted. Ask God to name any specific person or group in this category, and pray for them as He directs. Pray that radically real converts will be the result, and that powerful national and international ministries will emerge.

Release faith that your prayers are being answered now! *"The Lord is...patient with you, not wanting anyone to perish, but everyone to come to repentance"* (2 Peter 3:9). See also John 14:13–14 and John 16:24.

13. Ask God to name the major principalities over the nations and cities and wage spiritual warfare as directed by the Holy Spirit.

14. Finish by praising God, declaring faith in His promise.

"The nations will fear the name of the LORD, all the kings of the earth will revere your glory. For the LORD will rebuild Zion [His Church] and appear in his glory" (Psalm 102:15–16).

Declare that the purpose of all this intercession is that *"...all kingdoms on earth may know that you alone, O LORD, are God"* (2 Kings 19:19).

15. Keep on persisting in intercession. Don't let up.

"The watchman replies, 'Morning is coming, but also the night. If you would ask, then ask; and come back yet again' " [emphasis added] (Isaiah 21:12).

SUGGESTED PRAYER

Dear God,

I want to praise You for the many signs of Your mighty workings throughout the nations of the world. Praise Your name for the progress in unity, and the unprecedented vision and commitment of Your people to reach the unevangelized in this twentieth century. Hallelujah!

Give me greater vision and understanding of the importance of praying regularly for Your people, not only to shape the history of the nations, but also to be prepared to rule and reign with You throughout eternity. Show me the big picture. Deliver me from smallness of vision or thought. Thank You that You will.

In Jesus' name, Amen.

10

Praying for Spiritual Leaders

*F*or us to understand the importance of praying for spiritual leaders, we need to recognize a scriptural principle. God always works through God-appointed, anointed leadership to bring forth His maximum purposes. In Judges 5:2 and Psalm 110:3, God encourages us to expect that the people will follow this kind of leadership. If we're spiritually ambitious for the extension of God's kingdom, we'll need to take the application of this chapter seriously.

As God has shaped history around His people, the Church, He expects them to shape the history of each nation. Therefore, our main focus of prayer for leadership must always be on spiritual leaders. Satanic forces understand this importance, which is why spiritual leaders are particularly targeted. But our prayers can ward off and greatly help to diffuse interference from the enemy.

Leadership responsibility brings great privilege and accountability. James 3:1 makes it clear that because of the enormous influence they exert, teachers are judged by God with greater strictness. Teachers reproduce their own kind, and God doesn't want to multiply phonies. However, it's part of God's justice that spiritual leaders get more prayer support than others because of their additional responsibility and accountability.

When we perceive that a spiritual leader is in error, or has failed to meet our expectations, as a general rule, let us adopt the slogan, "Don't say it; pray it." Talk to the One who can correct the problem, not to the ones who could spread it.

In preparation for prayer for spiritual leaders, we need to ask God to reveal anything in us that would hinder effective prayer for them (Psalm 66:18.) For our prayers to be effective, we must have a forgiving spirit and a loving heart (Galatians 5:6).

We need to guard against a judgmental spirit or resentment toward leaders, asking God to flood our hearts with His love, and receiving it by faith (Romans 5:5).

SOME GUIDELINES TO GIVE FOCUS AND IMPACT TO OUR PRAYERS FOR SPIRITUAL LEADERS

Prayers That Help to Lighten Their Loads

1. Thank God for spiritual leaders and for the high price they've paid to be in leadership. It's always high.

We're instructed to honor our spiritual leaders. "*The elders who direct the affairs of the church well are worthy of double honor, especially those whose work is preaching and teaching*" (1 Timothy 5:17).

2. Pray that God will comfort and encourage spiritual leaders, and heal their wounded spirits and hurting hearts (Psalms 147:3).

So much pain results from the frequent pummeling and buffeting of criticism, misunderstandings, and untruths that are directed at them just because they're out front. It's part of the price to lead. Ask God to give these leaders grace and courage to endure.

Paul says; "*But in our trouble God has comforted us—and this, too, to help you: to show you from our personal experience how God will tenderly comfort you when you undergo these same sufferings. He will give you the strength to endure*" (2 Corinthians 1:6b–7 TLB). The Greek word for endure here means "remaining up under."

Plants wilt in my garden in the hot, summer afternoon sun. I water them, and then they remain up under the continued heat. When we pray like this, the Holy Spirit ministers to the leaders' wilted spirits, and they remain up under the heat of continued flak.

Colossians 1:11–12 promises endurance with joy: *"being strengthened with all power according to his glorious might so that you may have great endurance and patience, and joyfully giving thanks to the Father, who has qualified you to share in the inheritance of the saints in the kingdom of light."*

Since discouragement is one of Satan's strongest weapons against spiritual leaders, we need to be particularly vigilant about this prayer focus. How wonderful it would be if each reader would pause and pray, "Dear God, please bring to my mind the names of the leaders to whom you want me to express encouragement. Thank You that You will." Give Him time to speak. You, and they, will be blessed.

3. Ask God to pour out His supernatural grace and patience upon spiritual leaders.

Most leaders are under a heavy barrage of pressures related to their many and varied responsibilities. We can also ask God to reveal to us the pain of those pressures until we actually feel it in intercession. It means entering into the fellowship of their sufferings, and will help us guard against unnecessarily adding to those pressures.

We also need to ask God to give leaders the physical strength to endure as promised to all believers in Romans 8:11. We can pray that they will understand and appropriate the biblical truth that humility is the basic key to coping with pressure. *"God opposes the proud but gives grace to the humble"* (James 4:6b). Matthew 11:28–30 tells us that learning from Jesus' gentleness and humility will cause us to experience the truth that God's yoke is easy and His burden is light when we're weary and heavy laden.

4. We need to ask God to give leaders clear understanding that the underlying purpose in all their trials and testings is to conform them more to the likeness of the Lord Jesus (Romans 8:29) as they live in obedience to God's Word.

Pray for a release of God's mercy on the leaders, and that they will have a greater revelation of God's unfathomable love, absolute justice, and unswerving faithfulness to them in times of suffering (Deuteronomy 32:4).

5. Pray that wayward and fallen leaders will not only receive discipline in repentance and humility, but also have faith for their complete restoration and usefulness at the appropriate time.

David prayed; *"Let a righteous man strike me—it is a kindness; let him rebuke me—it is oil on my head. My head will not refuse it"* (Psalm 141:5).

We pray that the leaders involved in giving and receiving correction and discipline will be motivated by David's prayer: *"May integrity and uprightness protect me, because my hope is in you"* (Psalm 25:21).

We also pray that the following qualifications of leadership will be evidenced: *"He has showed you, O man, what is good. And what does the LORD require of you? To act justly and to love mercy and to walk humbly with your God"* (Micah 6:8).

Prayers Related to Spiritual Leaders' Personal Lives

1. Pray that spiritual leaders will find that their greatest fulfillment is in having a more intimate relationship with the Lord, rather than in ministry accomplishments.

Pray that worship and praise to the Lord will become an integral part of their lives.

Pray that leaders will make ministry to the Lord a priority over ministry to people (Luke 4:8).

We pray that they'll understand that submission and constant obedience to the Person of the Holy Spirit is the pathway of sustained power (Ephesians 5:18).

2. Pray that the fear of God will be upon spiritual leaders.

"To fear the LORD is to hate evil" (Proverbs 8:13a); *"through the fear of the LORD a man avoids evil"* (Proverbs 16:6b).

All fascination with sin or rationalization of sin comes from the lack of the hatred of sin. We sin for two basic reasons. We have a love for the sin, and we then choose to commit that sin.

The Bible says that the fear of the Lord is not only the beginning of knowledge and the beginning of wisdom, but also instruction in wisdom (Proverbs 15:33). Scripture also tells us that wisdom is absolutely essential for effective leadership. *"Wisdom makes one wise man more powerful than ten rulers in a city"* (Ecclesiastes 7:19).

The fear of the Lord is undoubtedly the greatest antidote for any immorality found among spiritual leaders. Let us therefore pray that a passion for holiness in thought, word, and deed will replace their love for self-gratification.

The fear of God is the only thing that will deliver spiritual leaders from that monster called the fear of man, which inevitably cripples their ability to move in spiritual authority. David's last words were highly significant to leadership:

"The Spirit of the Lord spoke through me; his word was on my tongue. The God of Israel spoke, the Rock of Israel said to me: 'When one rules over men in righteousness, when he rules in the fear of God, he is like the light of morning at sunrise on a cloudless morning, like the brightness after rain that brings the grass from the earth" (2 Samuel 23:2–4).

This means that when a leader's life is controlled by the hatred of sin, it is fresh and clean, brings light, life, and beauty, and is productive.

3. Pray that spiritual leaders will see the need to study God's character facet by facet, and His ways from His Word as a basis for their own lives, leadership, and teaching. Without this revelation, distortion of truth and unwise actions will result.

Pray that they will understand that all their academic and theological learning is no substitute for this course of training, in which there are no shortcuts. It takes time and diligence to study God's character and ways. God's perspective on this priority is emphasized in Proverbs 2:1–6. It's worthy of serious meditation.

Most leaders' spiritual problems stem from a lack of knowledge of either the character of God or His ways, or from disobedience to revealed truth. Some leaders can be trying to make God known to others without having taken time to know and understand Him themselves. We can understand and explain a person to others only to the degree we've taken time to know the person's character. It's the same in relation to God (Jeremiah 9:23–24).

4. Pray that spiritual leaders will be convinced by the Holy Spirit that it's more effective to speak to God on behalf of men than to speak to men on behalf of God.

Pray this so that they will be motivated to fulfill their priestly role of intercession and realize as Samuel the leader did that failure to do so is sinning against the Lord. *"God forbid that I should sin against the Lord in ceasing to pray for you"* (1 Samuel 12:23b KJV).

"Well done," will be said by the Lord to obedient leaders, not, "Well said."

A close study of the prayer life of Jesus as leader is the most enlightening and challenging thing I know in relation to the ministry of intercession.

5. Pray that all spiritual leaders will have vision for both worldwide revival and world evangelization, and be involved in intercession for them.

Pray that leaders will be prepared for the inevitable, awesome visitations of the Holy Spirit that accompany revival, and for the great end-time harvest of lost souls. *"The LORD will lay bare his holy arm in the sight of all the nations, and all the ends of the earth will see the salvation of our God"* (Isaiah 52:10).

Pray for leaders to have a deeper understanding of the ways of the Spirit in revival so that they will not resist His workings, particularly when those workings are unpredictable and unusual.

6. Pray that spiritual leaders will have a desire to be real, and have a holy hatred of hypocrisy, starting with themselves.

Pray this so that leaders will want to be transparent and honest, and will never project an image other than what God knows them to be. Pray that leaders will choose never to preach a truth unless they're living that truth; in other words, that their lives will validate their lips. Paul warns leaders against hypocrisy in Romans 2:21–27.

Ezra gives us the right priorities for those who teach; *"For Ezra had set his heart to study the law of the Lord, and to do it, and to teach his statutes and ordinances in Israel"* (7:10 RSV).

When sharing the truth it's not enough that we know and believe the truth; we must live the truth as well.

Paul's testimony rings with integrity: *"...I am sending to you Timothy, my son whom I love, who is faithful in the Lord. He will remind you of my way of life in Christ Jesus, which agrees with what I teach everywhere in every church"* (1 Corinthians 4:17).

My paraphrase of this scripture is, "Listen to what the one who knows me best says about my life. You'll then see that how I live is consistent with what I teach."

Pray also that God will powerfully convict all those who aren't real and honest and will bring them to repentance. Pray that God will expose those who resist His conviction. *"There is nothing concealed that will not be disclosed, or hidden that will not be made known"* (Luke 12:2); *"For God will bring every deed into judgment, including every hidden thing, whether it is good or evil"* (Ecclesiastes 12:14).

Nothing distorts the character of God more to the non-Christian than hypocritical spiritual leaders. The world will tolerate practically any sin in Christians except the sin of hypocrisy. Jesus wouldn't tolerate it either, and it was the subject of His strongest rebuke to religious leaders (Matthew 23:27–32).

7. Pray that God will reveal to spiritual leaders, and motivate them to act upon the truth, that only as they are truly submitted in spirit and actions to the authorities over them (Godward and manward) will God ever anoint them to lead and teach with authority, so that others will submit to their authority (Romans 13:1–6).

"Submitting yourselves one to another in the fear of God" (Ephesians 5:21 KJV). *"Obey your leaders and submit to their authority"* (Hebrews 13:17a).

8.   Ask God to give leaders a burning desire and spiritual ambition to be like Jesus, the greatest leader.

Pray that leaders will never forget that Jesus came primarily to seek and save that which was lost. Pray that God would increase their vision and prayer burden for reaching lost souls in the power of the Holy Spirit (Zechariah 4:6).

Pray that leaders will truly make the Lord Jesus Christ—not other spiritual leaders, whether biblical or not—their role model. Pray that each leader will resist the subtle temptation to encourage others to be molded into the leader's personal image instead of the Lord Jesus Christ.

One time when I was in Europe teaching at a training school, the Holy Spirit awakened me in the middle of the night with a simple but strong message that I was to deliver the next day to one of the male students. The young man had more than average potential for leadership, and was being discipled and mentored by a man of God who was a strong leader.

The message was: "Model your life only on the person of the Lord Jesus. If you model it on your earthly leader, you will be influenced by his weaknesses as well as his strengths. Only Jesus the Leader has no weaknesses." That young man received and heeded the word of the Lord and is today a strong leader over many people.

Only being like Jesus will release the manifestations of the strength of the Lion of the tribe of Judah and the meekness of the Lamb of God at the appropriate times. Both are necessary, and are made possible only through consistent submission and obedience to the Holy Spirit. *"To this you were called, because Christ suffered for you, leaving you an example, that you should follow in his steps"* (1 Peter 2:21).

9.   Pray that spiritual leaders will be kept from the folly of comparing themselves with other leaders and ministries.

"When they ...compare themselves with themselves, they are not wise" (2 Corinthians 10:12b). Ask God to show them that this only leads to pride, competitiveness, jealousy, criticism or intimidation, and insecurity.

10. Ask God to reveal to spiritual leaders any resentment or anger they may be harboring toward God or toward people for the price they have to pay to lead.

Ask God to reveal to them His absolute justice (Deuteronomy 32:4). Pray that they'll see that any bitterness in their spirits will become evident to others, and will thereby greatly lessen the impact of their leadership. *"See to it that no one misses the grace of God and that no bitter root grows up to cause trouble and defile many"* (Hebrews 12:15).

A leader with unresolved anger doesn't manifest peace and joy, and thereby gives a distorted view of God's character. *"Better a patient man than a warrior, a man who controls his temper than one who takes a city"* (Proverbs 16:32).

11. Ask God to purify spiritual leaders' motives and give them a passion only for God's glory in every situation.

Pray that God will bring leaders to the place where they die to their own reputation until they have the genuine, deep longing in their soul expressed by the psalmist: *"Not to us, O LORD, not to us but to your name be the glory, because of your love and faithfulness"* (Psalm 115:1).

Malachi 2:1–2 contains a strong warning to priests that if they will not take it to heart to give glory to God's name, God will curse what He has blessed. This warning calls for serious thought!

12. Pray that spiritual leaders will give needed correction and discipline with humility, mercy, and compassion, balanced with uncompromising firmness according to biblical standards.

"...correct, rebuke and encourage—with great patience and careful instruction" (2 Timothy 4:2b); *"Brothers, if someone is caught in a sin, you who are spiritual should restore him gently. But watch yourself, or you also may be tempted"* (Galatians 6:1).

Pray also that leaders in turn will receive needed correction and discipline in humility and repentance. *"He who listens to a life-giving rebuke will be at home among the wise"* (Proverbs 15:31).

Prayers Related to Spiritual Leaders' Ministries

1. Ask God to increase the flow of His love through spiritual leaders to their life partners, their children and grandchildren, and other relatives.

Pray that God will show leaders the importance of keeping their family relationships loving and close, and to never neglect their family at the expense of ministering to others. My dear mother used to often say, "Don't trample on the daisies while you're reaching for the dahlias." Wonderful advice for placing appropriate value and priority on the less spectacular things in life.

Ask God to show leaders that to minister in the love and life of the Lord Jesus to their family is the greatest privilege, opportunity, responsibility, challenge, and fulfillment (1 Timothy 5:8). *"Be sure you know the condition of your flocks, give careful attention to your herds"* (Proverbs 27:23). Pray that leaders will see that their first responsibility is to regularly intercede for their family.

2. Pray that spiritual leaders will have the humility to recognize that they're only one of a number of other ministry functions (some of which are outlined in Ephesians 4:11) and were never meant to "do it all."

Pray that they'll have the faith to release others to function in their complementary ministries (Romans 12:3–8). Scarcer and rarer than having ability is having the humility to recognize others' abilities and make room for them.

3. Ask God to bring spiritual leaders to a commitment to being unifiers in the Body of Christ, and to use them greatly as such.

According to John 17:23 unity is a vital key to world evangelization, and Psalm 133:1–3 tells us that God commands his blessing when we're experiencing the biblical standard of unity.

Soon after the Los Angeles riots in 1992, Dr. Lloyd Ogilvie, then pastor of Hollywood Presbyterian Church, and Pastor Ken Ulmer from Faith Missionary Baptist Church (from the riot-devastated area of Los Angeles), along with some members of the congregations, joined with Pastor Jack Hayford and many of us at The Church on The Way in Van Nuys, California, for a Sunday night service. The manifest presence of the living Christ was absolutely awesome. I believe that this was a direct result of the deeper levels of humility, love and commitment to one another that were openly expressed by these three spiritual leaders who had been close friends for years. Subsequently, new levels of unity were experienced in these congregations. The sense of God's approving presence was so strong that I didn't want that service to end.

We need to pray that an outpouring of God's Spirit in humility, love, and reconciliation would come and dissolve all ethnic, denominational, gender, and cultural differences. Pride, prejudice and sectarianism cannot survive in the rarified atmosphere of God's pure love. Radically real reconciliation is taking place in unprecedented proportions among leaders in many parts of the world in answer to much prayer.

4. Pray that God will reveal to spiritual leaders all sins of presumption.

Many times during David's leadership, he failed to wait on God and moved in presumption, which inevitably brought confusion and suffering to those he led. We find David praying a significant prayer, *"Keep back Your servant also from presumptuous sins; Let them not have dominion over me. Then...I shall be innocent of great transgression"* (Psalm 19:13 NKJV).

Jesus came, among other things, to show us how to live (1 John 2:6), and He never did anything independently of the Father (John 5:19, 30; John 8:26, 38). Pray that leaders will have the humility to wait on God for directions in matters large and small (unless there's the immediate witness of the Holy Spirit as to the course of action).

Pray that spiritual leaders will not accept speaking engagements and other commitments unless clearly directed by the Holy Spirit. *"For the one whom God has sent speaks the words of God"* (John 3:34a). Pray also that they'll never speak other than the specific word of the Lord for each occasion that they preach and teach.

"But which of them has stood in the council of the LORD *to see or to hear his word? Who has listened and heard his word? I did not send these prophets, yet they have run with their message; I did not speak to them, yet they have prophesied. But if they had stood in my council, they would have proclaimed my words to my people and would have turned them from their evil ways and from their evil deeds"* (Jeremiah 23:18, 21–22).

We also need to discharge our responsibility in interceding for the word of the Lord to be released to these leaders—and not leave all that responsibility to them, or take for granted that they get it quickly and easily.

5. Stand in the gap for spiritual leaders against the forces of darkness.

Our high praises to God drive back the enemy and diffuse his power (2 Chronicles 20:22; Psalm 149:5–9). We go into spiritual combat, commanding the forces of darkness to cease their assault on leaders:

- In the name of the Lord Jesus Christ (Philippians 2:9–11).
- Wielding the sword of the Spirit, which is the Word of God (Ephesians 6:17; 1 John 3:8).
- Presenting the shed blood of the Lord Jesus with the word of our testimony (Revelation 12:11).
- In the power of the Holy Spirit (Zechariah 4:6).

Pray that God will unmask the enemy wherever he's working by giving leaders revelation of his tactics.

6. Finally, ask God to show spiritual leaders that it's how they finish that counts.

There's a high price for a sustained anointing in ministry and intimate friendship with God. It's the price of obedience. But the rewards from God far outweigh the price. Pray that leaders will understand this, and out of passionate love for the Lord Jesus be motivated to pay the price.

SUGGESTED PRAYER

Father God,

I pray that as I diligently make application of this message on an ongoing basis, the spiritual leaders among the nations will hear You say to them in a coming day, "Well done good and faithful servant. Enter into the joy of your Lord." Thank You that You will do it for Your great name's sake. Amen.

11

Praying for the Conversion of Leaders in Authority and Influence

Having established the priority of praying for spiritual leaders in the previous chapter, we now look at other important aspects of leadership.

Leaders function in two main categories: authority and influence. People follow both. The president or prime minister in a nation has great authority, while film stars have great influence. The mass media in general have enormous influence to shape people's thinking and subsequent actions. When we understand that God wants righteous leaders serving in both categories, we get to cooperate with Him in unusual and exciting prayer adventures.

We see from the Bible how God delights in promoting and establishing righteous leadership in a nation. Because of this, we have a responsibility to pray consistently for righteous leaders to be placed in positions of authority and influence in every nation, as salt and light (Proverbs 29:2). The following leaders were powerfully used of God to alter the course of their nation's history.

Joseph became second in authority to the reigning pharaoh in Egypt and instructed his leaders in wisdom.

Daniel became third in command to the reigning monarch of Babylon and exercised his prophetic ministry under four kings. Both men were prepared by God for their positions of authority from their youth.

Mordecai became next in authority to the king of Persia.

Nehemiah was authorized by King Artaxerxes to take a leave of absence from the palace to carry out God's mandate to lead God's people at a crucial time in their history.

Deborah, as a judge and prophetess, led Israel with righteous authority.

Queen **Esther**, as wife of the king of Persia, exercised great and godly influence in her nation.

God always has His chosen men and women in place at the right time. But what about unrighteous leaders in authority and influence in the nations? Is God interested in them? Do we as intercessors have a part to play in altering the course of their lives, and the fulfilling of their destinies? This is where a prayer adventure starts.

When Richard Nixon was the president of the United States, Chuck Colson was known as "the hatchet man" among a group of men close to the president. Colson matched the title well as a hard-hitting, unchurched, successful lawyer who was involved in the Watergate scandal. He was subsequently imprisoned for over a year—seemingly one of the most impossible-to-be-converted people in America at that time.

However, before going to prison, Colson became exposed to the genuine love, fellowship, prayers, and consistent Christian witness of a group of men in Washington, D.C. After some time, Chuck Colson found the strong force of the Holy Spirit's influence to be irresistible. One night, as he sat behind the wheel of his car, Colson broke down and wept before God. He gave up the right to do his own thing and capitulated to a new Commander-in-Chief—the President of heaven and earth! Colson's life story, including his remarkable conversion is detailed in his first book *Born Again*.[1]

---

1. by Chosen Books, 1976

He not only has authored a number of other outstanding Christian books, but also has founded Prison Fellowship, an organization that brings the gospel, Bible teaching, and fellowship to prisoners in many countries.

Back in the early 1970s, Jim and I had been directed by the Holy Spirit during our weekly prayer times together for America to pray that God would bring about the conversion of a prominent and influential man operating in Washington D.C. in the top government circles of the United States. We had no idea who that might be. Our persistent, fervent, expectant prayers were not answered in a hurry. But we never lagged in our pursuit of God to land a "big fish"—one whose testimony would affect the nations.

We've never doubted that Chuck Colson was the one God had in mind when He gave us the vision and burden for this interesting and strategic project. It would be consistent with God's ways that other intercessors (possibly many) were given the same direction in prayer during those years.

Here is a story from another point on the social scale.

I had just been interviewed on a Christian television program when I noted with interest that the guest following me was an ex-leader in the mafia who had one of the most amazing stories of conversion I've ever heard. You can read about it in his fascinating book, *Tell It to the Mafia*[2] by Joe de Nato.

Later I questioned him. "Joe, who prayed for you? To have had such a radical conversion, someone must have been praying for you. A grandmother?"

"No, I've not had the slightest Christian influence in my heritage. I know of nobody on planet Earth who would have prayed for me," he replied.

I persisted. "Joe there is a spiritual law that just as in natural birth there is always travail, so in spiritual birth. Someone has to have prevailed in prayer for you."

2. by Logos International, 1975

Then the Holy Spirit nudged me. "Ask him when he was converted."

"When did you have that incredible transforming experience with the living Christ?"

"About five years ago."

I made a memory check and recalled that it was exactly five years before during a time of intercession for America, that I was first directed to pray for leading men in the mafia to be converted. I had continued to intercede for these desperately needy men. Now, not only was God letting me see one who had been transformed from an all-out criminal life to become a born-again Christian, but also Joe de Nato had become a full-time evangelist, radiating the love and life of Christ to all with whom he came in contact. I know firstand.

The next morning, I discovered Joe in a restaurant witnessing to a waitress about God's love for her, even before she took his order! I felt a renewed challenge about my burden for the lost. This man's leadership abilities were now being channeled into influencing many more people toward righteousness than they had been toward evil.

I had a similar experience some years ago. I was having a time of intercession for America when God directed me to pray for leading homosexual men and women. It was a Saturday night, the last week in October. Two years later, while teaching on television on the subject of intercession, I shared something of the burden the Lord had given me for homosexuals. A young woman who was watching the program that day found out where I was speaking that night, came to the meeting, and afterwards shared her story with me.

Thirty-one years old, the woman had been an all-out leading lesbian. She and her partner were held up as a model relationship among her homosexual associates. "Look, it works. This couple is proof," it had always been said if them. Then in quite a remarkable way the woman heard the gospel and was converted.

After months of loving, patient counseling and much prayer, she was completely healed in mind, body, soul, and spirit and set free from the bondage of thirteen years of sexual perversion.

"When were you converted?" I asked her.

"Two years ago."

"What month?"

"October."

"What week?"

"The last..."

Again it was the exact time God had first burdened me to pray for leading homosexuals in the United States to be converted. This woman went into full-time service for the Lord and was used to reach many for Christ.

God delights to give us these kinds of encouragement in His time. When the disciples asked Jesus, *"Who then can be saved?"* He responded, *"With man this is impossible, but with God all things are possible"* (Matthew 19:25b–26b).

No matter how unlikely to be converted a person appears, we must always remember Jesus' response to that question. A city of Samaritans was evangelized through the conversion of a woman with a seamy past (John 4). A dishonest tax collector was hardly the most likely candidate to become one of Jesus' followers (Luke 19:8–10).

The testimony of a delivered demoniac was used to spread the gospel in ten cities (Mark 5:20).

The only category of people Jesus said were more difficult than others to reach with the gospel were the wealthy. Sadly, I think that instead of our having more concern for their lost souls and directing more prayer and more love towards them, they are often the ones who receive the least attention.

The rich are among the most insecure people in the world because they are seldom sure whom they can really trust. This immediately presents a challenge to serious intercessors. How about asking God to lay a wealthy person on your heart, and pray consistently for that person's conversion?

It is certainly not difficult for God to reveal Himself to any soul. God has numberless ways of doing this.

Because God says, *"Righteousness exalts a nation"* (Proverbs 14:34a), will you commit yourself to God on a regular basis to pray that righteous leaders be placed in the areas of the Church, the government, the judicial system, education, business and commerce, the medical profession, the media, sports, the arts, and entertainment?

"No one from the east or the west or from the desert can exalt a man. But it is God who judges: He brings one down, he exalts another" (Psalm 75:6–7).

Will you ask God to lay some seemingly impossible-to-be-converted people in leadership on your heart, and believe God for their conversions? If you do, you will capture the thrill and the prospect of the eternal purposes that are involved.

12

Praying for the World's Unevangelized

A s with all other forms of intercession, our intercession for the unevangelized must start with God. We need to see the unreached millions from God's perspective, from His thoughts, His heart, His reactions, His purposes. God has great love and compassion and longs for the friendship of the unreached, with plans to bring about their conversion.

God is fully aware that from the desire of the unreached to worship Him, because they were created in His likeness and image, they've turned to what was presented to them as truth.

He is equally aware that most are blinded from the real truth and are held in the bondage of religiosity and fear by the enemy of their souls, Satan. Many of the unevangelized are under the influence or control of the most subtle of all Satan's emissaries—religious principalities.

God, however, is totally unimpressed with Satan's power over and plans for the world's one and one-quarter billion unevangelized. He has already paid the full price for their deliverance and freedom and has defeated their captor at the cross.

God knows that the power of the Holy Spirit is infinitely greater than the power of the religious spirits. In fact, He has limitless ways that we've never heard or thought of to reveal Himself to the unreached.

In a country of West Africa in an area inhabited by ardent Muslims, ten men were sitting in a circle, chanting the name of Allah to work themselves into a trance. They believed that the spirit of Mohammed would come and perch on the piece of cloth that lay in the center of the circle. Instead, the cloth disappeared, and the men heard a voice say, "This is not the way. Follow Me." The men were all shocked and abruptly ended their seance. After returning home, all ten of them individually saw a vision of the Lord Jesus. Subsequently, they all went to a local Christian pastor asking to be taught about Jesus Christ.

Another interesting account is taken from George Otis, Jr.'s article *The Holy Spirit around the World* from *Charisma and Christian Life Magazine*, January 1993:

> Some individuals living in the isolated reaches of the Sahara Desert continue to have visions of the Lord and to request Scriptures so that they might learn more about Christ.
>
> In Egypt, a high ranking military officer and devout Muslim was visited by Jesus in a dream. Upon waking, he immediately sought out Christians in his unit to see if they could provide him with a copy of God's Word. Finding only one believer in his officer corps, he quietly asked if he could borrow the man's Bible. In a manner reminiscent of Annanias' reluctant ministrations to Saul, the surprised Christian cautiously agreed to the Muslim officer's request. As a result, after several days of pouring over the gospels, the officer decided to become a disciple of Jesus. In the months that...followed (according to reports out of Cairo), this man [became] the same kind of bold witness that Saul/Paul became after the blindness was lifted from his eyes.

God is committed to giving the unevangelized multitudes the opportunity of coming into His kingdom, so much so that

He won't release His Son to return again until they've all had a chance to hear the gospel. *"And this gospel of the kingdom will be preached in the whole world as a testimony to all nations, and then the end will come"* (Matthew 24:14).

God's main strategy is to bring His people to think about and react as He does, to the unevangelized. Out of our love for Him first, we are to cooperate with His plans to pray for, evangelize, and disciple the unreached.

WHO ARE THEY? AND WHERE ARE THEY?

The world's unevangelized are made up primarily of Muslims, Hindus, and Buddhists living in what is called "the 10/40 window," the area between ten degrees north and forty degrees north of the equator in a belt that extends from West Africa across Asia. The area represents:

- **The Middle East**, in such countries as Afghanistan, Saudi Arabia, Iran, Iraq, and Kuwait.
- **North Africa**, in countries like Libya, Algeria, and Mauritania.
- **Asia**, in such countries as Pakistan and India.

Fifty-five of the sixty-two countries in this region of the world are among the least evangelized, constituting 95 percent of the one and one-quarter billion who have not heard God's plan of salvation.

God's priority plan to reach the unevangelized is the mobilization of His people in united prayer. We are to pray with clean hearts, according to His will and His ways from His Word, in faith, energized by the Holy Spirit.

In recent years, God's people worldwide have cooperated with God's plan as never before in history. In 1996, 35,367,122 intercessors are on record as having participated in a massive, concentrated thrust targeted at praying for the unreached people in the 10/40 window, referred to as "Praying through the Window II." This included the involvement of 143,447 churches and 8,146 ministries. Six hundred and seven prayer journeys were taken by people who went into the 10/40 region to pray on site. Millions more are being mobilized globally to participate in the 1997 "Praying through the Window III" project.

Praying for the unevangelized involves three main prayer focuses.

THE FIRST PRAYER FOCUS NEEDS TO BE ON GOD'S PEOPLE WORLDWIDE

1. Worship and praise God, thanking Him for what He's already done in these countries. Praise releases God's power.

Keeping our focus on God's position, power, purpose, and plans for the unevangelized nations helps us to believe that, "...*the one who is in you is greater than the one who is in the world*" (1 John 4:4b).

- God's **position** in relation to the unevangelized nations: "*How awesome is the* LORD *Most High, the great King over all the earth! God reigns over the nations; God is seated on his holy throne*" (Psalm 47:2, 8).

- God's **power** over the unevangelized nations: "*He makes nations great, and destroys them; he enlarges nations, and disperses them*" (Job 12:23);

    "*The* LORD *will lay bare his holy arm in the sight of all the nations, and all the ends of the earth will see the salvation of our God*" (Isaiah 52:10).

- God's **purpose** and **plans** for the unevangelized nations: "...*with your blood you purchased men for God from every tribe and language and people and nation*" (Revelation 5:9b); "*All the ends of the earth will remember and turn to the* LORD, *and all the families of the nations will bow down before him, for dominion belongs to the* LORD *and he rules over the nations*" (Psalm 22:27–28).

Taking time to meditate on the above six scriptures greatly increases our faith.

2. Humble ourselves before God and identify with the sins of omission in the Body of Christ in relation to the unevangelized millions.

We say, like Daniel, "I and my people have sinned." We confess our indifference, our ignorance about the unreached generally, our lack of love, lack of concern for their lostness, blindness, and bondage, and our resultant prayerlessness. We repent if the sins are personal, and make a commitment to pray regularly for the unreached.

3. Ask God to have mercy on us and His people (Habakkuk 3:2).

4. Pray that God will unite the Body of Christ, as unity is the greatest factor to influence the lost to commit their lives to Christ (John 17:23).

We pray for God to convict His people of the pride and prejudice that separates them, and that we'll realize that without unity we will be ineffective. *"Every city or household divided against itself will not stand"* (Matthew 12:25b).

5. Pray that God will stir His people worldwide in relation to the unreached, and cause them to have His heart and mind toward the unevangelized.

"The Lord is...not wanting anyone to perish, but everyone to come to repentance" (2 Peter 3:9).

6. Ask God to raise up an army of intercessors from every nation who, empowered by the Holy Spirit, will pray on a regular basis for the unreached (Psalm 2:8–9; Ephesians 5:18).

7. Ask God to raise up visionaries who will seek Him for strategies of how to reach the unevangelized.

Pray that they'll be alerted to the neglected areas, and the "strategic time" opportunities, for an extraordinary harvest (Proverbs 29:18).

8. Pray that those who have received vision and are implementing it will be encouraged, and heard worldwide, and supported.

9. Ask God to thrust forth laborers into the harvest fields of the unevangelized nations, and especially from the fivefold ministries mentioned in Ephesians 4:11.

Pray that all will be motivated to fulfill the conditions to be empowered by the Holy Spirit (Ephesians 5:18).

10. Pray that God will call and enable His people to learn the languages of the people groups who don't have the Bible, translate them into their languages, and get them into the hands of the unevangelized.

"The unfolding of your words gives light..." (Psalm 119:130a).

11. Ask God to increase the spiritual effectiveness of the media ministries worldwide that are targeted at the unevangelized: radio, television, audio and video cassettes, films, correspondence, literature, etc.

An encouraging, recent report of answered prayer as a result of the fifth annual global 30 Days Muslim Prayer Focus, comes from the U.S. Headquarters of the missionary radio group H.C.J.B: "We have seen increased response to short-wave broadcasts; reports of clear reception in areas where it was previously only fair, and many new opportunities for 'radio planting' in restricted countries. God is opening doors miraculously with government permits, finances, local partners and missionary staff. We have seen an increased focus and enthusiasm for providing radio for Muslim-dominated countries."

12. Ask God to raise up ministries that are targeted at youth and children (Matthew 19:14; Mark 9:36).

Satanic forces are targeting these age groups as never before.

THE SECOND PRAYER FOCUS IS ON THE BODY OF CHRIST WITHIN THE LARGELY UNEVANGELIZED AREAS

We must never presume there are no believers in any area of the world. *"In the past, he let all nations go their own way. Yet he has not left himself without testimony..."* (Acts 14:16–17a).

1. Pray that God will encourage, protect, empower, strengthen, make bold, and deliver His people, even if there's only a remnant.

"...pray for the remnant that still survives" (2 Kings 19:4b). Special focus should be on the persecuted and imprisoned

(Hebrews 13:3). The following story is taken from George Otis, Jr.'s book *The Last of the Giants*:[1]

> During some of the worst years of the brutal Mengistu regime in Ethiopia, miracles not only brought many into the Kingdom of God, they kept some people out of the grave as well.
>
> On one occasion in the early 1980s, an Ethiopian evangelist was arrested by revolutionary guards in the act of preaching and was taken at gunpoint to a house for interrogation. After the questioning had begun, one of the political officers asked mockingly: "So you believe in God. Do you think he will save you from us?"
>
> The guards then lifted their prisoner up on top of a table, and unscrewed a bulb from the ceiling light socket. The evangelist was then given the choice of putting his finger in the live socket or being summarily shot. Knowing the officers were serious, he placed his finger in the socket and cried out, "In the name of Jesus!"
>
> Instantly, all the lights went out in the entire district. At this, the Communist guards climbed fearfully under the table while the evangelist stood praising God. While the officials could only meekly command him to curtail his preaching, not surprisingly, they found him at it again the very next day. This time he was then taken and beaten with thorns, and like the Apostle Stephen during his stoning, saw a vision of the Lord. The evangelist did not feel the pain. After this beating he became even more zealous for the Kingdom in Ethiopia.

2. Pray that God will show the believers how essential biblical unity is (John 17:23; Mark 11:25).

---

1. by Baker Books, 1991

3. Pray that all Christians will have access to the Word of God, be empowered by the Holy Spirit, walk in the fear of the Lord, and multiply as they share their faith.

"Then the church...was strengthened; and encouraged by the Holy Spirit, it grew in numbers, living in the fear of the Lord" (Acts 9:31); *"Day after day, in the temple courts and from house to house, they never stopped teaching and proclaiming the good news that Jesus is the Christ"* (Acts 5:42).

4. Pray for an unprecedented outpouring of the Holy Spirit on the believers.

We pray that in turn they will be given vision to pray persistently for true revival, be spiritually prepared, and be used by God when He answers (Joel 2:15–17; Acts 1:14).

5. Pray that God will raise up righteous leaders, and put them into all spheres of authority and influence in the nation (Proverbs 28:12).

Joseph, Daniel, Mordecai, and Esther are encouraging biblical examples. Ask God to raise up from the newly converted, anointed apostles, prophets, evangelists, pastors, and teachers as outlined in Ephesians 4:11. This kind of praying is being dramatically answered.

A missionary friend of mine tells about recently meeting a converted Hindu priest in a nation that is aggressively opposed to Christianity. He relayed the priest's story of being tortured, beaten, and arrested numerous times and how he had trekked to virtually every district of the country and succeeded in planting over five hundred cell groups of believers. "Fear and faith do not mix" he said. "We have suffered and paid the price and now we're claiming this nation for Jesus Christ."

6. Pray that God's people in the unevangelized areas will study the Bible to understand the character and ways of God (Proverbs 2:1–5) and consistently live what they believe and teach.

Paul's testimony is a shining example of this kind of integrity (I Corinthians 4:17).

7. Pray that believers will be given world vision, be involved in intercession for the rest of the world, and be

ready to obey the Great Commission (Isaiah 56:7; Romans 10:14–15).

THE THIRD PRAYER FOCUS IS ON THE LOST IN THE LARGELY UNEVANGELIZED NATIONS

1. **Pray that God will stir the lost in their spirits, motivating them to seek the higher power they already know exists (Romans 1:19–20).**

Pray that God will prepare their hearts to receive the gospel when they hear it (Acts 10:33–35). Pray that He will continue to use the redemptive analogies that are woven into their culture and folklore that point to the gospel, as described in Don Richardson's book *Peace Child*.[2]

2. **Pray that God will give the lost a revelation of the Lord Jesus as the Son of God, and of His unconditional love for them.**

Reports continue to flow in from many parts of the world of Muslims and other unevangelized peoples having revelations of the Lord Jesus as the Son of God, with subsequent conversions. Some of these are Christian missionaries today. The following thrilling report comes from Keith and Kim Greig, coordinators of 30 Days Muslim Prayer Focus International:

> 1 August 1996. During the 1996 30 Day Muslim Prayer Focus over five million Christians worldwide participated in praying for the Muslim World. Over 300,000 prayer guides were distributed in 25 languages from 30 regional offices. We have received hundreds of incredible testimonies of miracles, visions, dreams and Muslims coming to Christ as a direct result. Equally exciting are the many letters from Christians who write of how God has changed their hearts towards Muslims from fear to love and

---

2. by Regal Books, 1974

compassion, and a new desire to reach out to them with the Gospel of Jesus.

It is fascinating to discover stories that illustrate the uniqueness of the way God brings the revelation of the gospel to the unevangelized. One of them comes from Greg Fisher, who is a missionary in Ghana with the International Foursquare denomination. Greg and some fellow missionaries were focusing on reaching the large village of Wasa Japa. A breakthrough started when an African pastor of one of the Foursquare churches, Nathaniel Donkor, a former herbalist and fetish priest, witnessed to one of the subchiefs about the salvation he had found in Jesus Christ. This occurred when the two were riding together on a bus and the subchief was reading a Muslim book with a title something like *Why No One Should Ever Consider Being a Christian*. Nathaniel's witness resulted in the subchief's conversion to Christ.

About three months prior to the outreach to the Wasa Japa people, Nathaniel had led his small congregation in extended times of fasting and prayer. Greg Fisher also wrote to all his supporters in the United States asking them to fast and pray in anticipation of reaching these unevangelized people. This resulted in the chief's inviting the missionaries to come and speak to his village about Jesus Christ. The chief then declared himself a follower of Christ and demonstrated to the village his commitment by being baptized in water. At the end of the outreach, about one hundred twenty people had made the same commitment, including elderly men and women who had been lifelong idol worshipers. Entire extended families came to Christ at one time.

Repeatedly the people would tell the missionaries the same story of having a dream and hearing a voice (the Holy Spirit) saying the same words to each one: "Foursquare is coming. They will have an important message for you. This is what you have been waiting for all your life." They hadn't any idea what "Foursquare" meant, but they were anticipating something very beneficial, to say the least.

When the missionaries identified themselves to the chief as belonging to the Foursquare denomination, the chief and the people were thoroughly prepared to hear the good news of the gospel. On the last day of their visit to that village, the missionaries were summoned to the palace of the head chief, along with the three chiefs, the entire royal family (some of whom were Folk Muslims), and the village elders. The missionaries were given a gift of two acres of land for the purpose of establishing a church in their village.

3. Pray that God will bring a great spiritual awakening among the people as they become exposed to the gospel, whether through Christian media, the Bible, or individual believers.

Pray that the people's minds will be illuminated, their spirits pierced, and their wills motivated to act upon the truth of the provision for their salvation through committing their lives to the Lord Jesus Christ.

Believe the promise: *"For as the soil makes the sprout come up and a garden causes seeds to grow, so the Sovereign LORD will make righteousness and praise spring up before all nations"* (Isaiah 61:11). Phenomenal reports continue to flow in from around the world of multiplied thousands coming to Christ through the *Jesus Film* project of Campus Crusade for Christ International.

4. Pray that God will open people's minds to see the falseness and futility of their religions and ideologies, and become aware that Christianity is the only religion that can change a person's heart (2 Corinthians 5:17).

It is happening. Many missionary organizations, churches and ministries worldwide are experiencing an unprecedented harvest of unconverted coming to Christ.

5. Pray that God will reveal Himself to unrighteous leaders in positions of authority and influence and bring them to salvation.

A recent president of Togo, Africa, for example, was converted while in office. We pray that God will overthrow those who persistently resist conviction, and put righteous leaders in their place (Psalm 75:6–7). The Philippines and Panama are two areas where this has resulted.

6. Prepare for spiritual warfare.

Ask God to name the principalities that dominate the minds of the lost in the country or people groups, and then engage in spiritual warfare. Come against those principalities in the name of the Lord Jesus Christ, quoting Scriptures that give believers authority over the enemy, and presenting Jesus' shed blood by which the principalities are defeated (Ephesians 6:10–18).

Enter into sustained fervent praise to God for His victory over satanic strongholds. Praise releases God's power (Psalm 47:1–3; Psalm 44:4–8). Keep in mind that:

- Light is more powerful than darkness.
- Truth is stronger than error.
- There's more grace in God's heart than sin in men's hearts.
- There's more power in the Holy Spirit to convict men of sin, than the power of satanic forces to tempt men to sin.
- There's more power in one drop of the shed blood of the Lord Jesus Christ to cleanse men's hearts from the stain of sin, than the accumulated filth of men's sin since Adam and Eve.

SUGGESTED PRAYER

Almighty God,

I desperately need to have far more of Your perspective on the world's unevangelized people. I submit to the Holy Spirit's working in my life to bring that about. As I pray consistently, according to Your priorities and ways from Your Word, for the millions that are yet to be reached with the gospel, I believe You will meet my need and theirs.

Thank You for Your great mercy, power, and love which makes all this possible.

In Jesus' name, Amen.

13

Satan's Challenge to the Body of Christ

Satanic forces challenge the Church today with regard to the unevangelized just as they did to God's people through Sennacherib, the evil king of Assyria, when Hezekiah was king of Judah (see Isaiah 36).

Satan today says in effect, "Where has there been a major breakthrough in Christianity among the millions of Muslims, Buddhists, and Hindus? They've always been under my domination and control, and always will be" (verses 18–22). Satan even has the audacity to tell us not to believe anything anyone—not even God—says to the contrary (verses 13–18). Millions of Christians believe Satan and do nothing. They have become impressed with Satan's limited power and therefore are intimidated by it.

The subtlety by which religious spirits operate is revealed when the enemy of the souls of mankind quotes God as his source of authority: "*The* LORD *himself told me to march against this country and destroy it*" (verse 10).

Perhaps Satan's greatest challenge to God's people comes when he says that he will even supply us with the means—if we can come up with the manpower dedicated enough to stand against his superior forces. "*Come now, make a bargain with my master, the king of Assyria: I will give you two thousand horses—if you can put riders on them!"* (verse 8). Only our obedience to the Great Commission matches that challenge.

I'm always fascinated with God's response to Satan's threats and challenges to God's people. In this story, God simply sent one angel on an expedition to wipe out 185,000 soldiers in the Assyrian army in one night while the people of God were sleeping soundly (Isaiah 37:36). I have written in my Bible, "No big deal to God."

The response of the Body of Christ to Satan must align with the Word of God. We must see our enemy solely from God's perspective. Satan is nothing but a fallen angel doomed to eternal destruction (Isaiah 14:12; Revelation 20:10).

Because of Jesus' shed blood on the cross, Satan's activity is illegal, and his claims invalid (Colossians 2:15). The full price for the lost to be freed from satanic bondage has been paid by the Lord Jesus (Hebrews 2:14–15). However, in all honesty and humility, we have to agree with Satan to our shame that in the past there hasn't been a major breakthrough among the millions of yet unevangelized peoples. We, the Church, have largely let these people remain under satanic domination. We confess that *"We have not brought salvation to the earth; we have not given birth to people of the world"* (Isaiah 26:18b).

We take the blame. But…because of God's position, power, purpose, and plans related to the nations, God will prevail, and unprecedented history will yet be made among those very people who have not yet heard the gospel.

God continues to stir His people worldwide in a diversity of ways to become active participants in the battle for their souls—on the offensive rather than the defensive. Unparalleled changes for the advancing of God's kingdom are taking place. For example, YWAM founder Loren Cunningham reported that in Indonesia alone, nineteen million people switched from Islam to Christianity during the decade of the 1980s. He also shared that in Singapore, between 1989 and 1995, the number of Christians increased from 10 percent to 12 percent of the total population. And 45 percent of the student community are now Christians, as are 80 percent of the medical community. Loren further stated the significant statistic that in 1995, one in seven people in the world were said to be born again believers. These are some of many radical advancements in the kingdom of God.

DIFFICULT FOR WHOM?

We must never even think that it's difficult for God to convert Muslims, Hindus, Buddhists, Shintoists, atheists, humanists, animists, and tribal groups. *"I am the LORD, the God of all mankind. Is anything too hard for me?"* (Jeremiah 32:27). When the disciples asked the Lord Jesus who could be saved, Jesus' response was, *"What is impossible with men is possible with God"* (Luke 18:27b). Therefore, if it's not difficult for God, it is only difficult in the minds of unbelieving Christians. Our unbelief can be one of the greatest hindrances to the salvation of millions of souls. *"And he did not do many miracles there because of their lack of faith"* (Matthew 13:58).

Remember, God hears prayer. He answers faith. Satanic forces are not going to hinder millions of the yet unevangelized from coming to Christ. Jesus said, *"...I will build my church, and the gates of Hades will not overcome it"* (Matthew 16:18b).

GOD IS BREAKING THROUGH

Intercessors have been praying in faith for many years for God to sovereignly reveal Himself to the unevangelized. Never before have the answers to such prayer been more evident than today.

The following stories are some of many that illustrate this fact.

From Buddhism

My family is Buddhist. My grandfather was a prominent figure in the foremost Buddhist organization in our country. My father, a kind, intellectual person who chose to be an atheist, sent me to Buddhist schools. Growing up, I participated in traditional Buddhist ceremonies, meditating and reciting stanzas in the temple and at home. Seven years prior to my coming to the United States I had a very distinct dream. I was standing near the ocean with a few other people. It was nighttime. A figure clothed in a long, white garment appeared from the misty darkness. He walked towards us with cupped hands in which He held water. When He stopped near me, He poured the water on my face and said, "You are purified." After that He sat down next to me and held my hand, filling me with an overwhelming sense of peace, comfort, and strength. When I woke up my face was wet with tears. I was very aware that this person was Jesus Christ.

Three months after I came to the United States I heard the message of the gospel, and how the Lord Jesus loved me and wanted me to give my life to Him. My heart, already prepared by the dream, received Him gladly.

This intelligent, attractive, spiritual young woman had formerly lived in the 10/40 window region. She was one of 250 from my home church, The Church on The Way in Southern California, who went out in the summer of 1993 on one of nineteen world teams to evangelize in eighteen overseas countries. Be encouraged as you pray for millions more like her to be converted.

From Islam

Recently, a former Muslim told an American missionary friend in Central Asia, that during a business trip, he had dreams and visions of the Lord Jesus five nights in a row that subsequently led to his conversion.

The following story appeared in the Global Harvest Ministries (Colorado) October 1995 *Prayer Track News*:

In a Muslim country, a rich man brought his very sick daughter who had been paralyzed for 4 years to a Christian hospital. They put her in a private room which had a cross hanging on the wall. The father, a very devout Muslim, demanded that the cross be taken down at once. The cross was removed because the Christian staff were threatened for witnessing in a Muslim country. That evening, a Christian nurse quietly told the sick girl that Jesus Christ died on the cross for her sins and would forgive her sins, and could heal her.

The girl could not sleep that night because she had so many questions. "He can heal me? Who is He and where is He??? What is this mystery of the cross? Why was my father so angry and so afraid of this cross?" She longed to know more about Isa (Jesus). In the quiet of that night, she saw a figure clothed in white. He had a halo of light around His head that filled the whole room. Then she heard His voice, "Get up and put the cross back on the wall." With fear and trembling she said, "I cannot walk." Jesus then revealed Himself to her and told her, "I am Jesus who died on the cross, but I am alive. Get up and walk." She got up and took the cross from under her bed and put it back on the wall. Then she turned, but the Lord was no longer there. Realizing what had just happened, she started shouting, "I saw Isa and He healed me! I can walk, I can walk!" She called her father who rushed to the hospital and witnessed what had happened. With tears in his eyes, all he could say was, "I want to know more about Jesus."

From Atheism

Albania has been and still is one of the most challenging, interesting, and thrilling prayer projects—especially as it relates to Satan's challenge to the Church. This tiny nation of over three million people had boasted for decades of being the most atheistic nation in the world. It was among the most opposed to Christianity, and believers were subject to extreme persecution and deprivation. Some Christians were put in barrels and rolled into the sea. To be found even turning the radio dial to anything other than an Albanian Communist station could mean being reported on and imprisoned for both Christians and non-Christians .

The more Satan tried to intimidate the Church by his roar, the more a number of intercessors who were scattered throughout the world prayed for a complete reversal of Satan's plans for Albania. As the decades passed, we knew it was only a matter of time before the boastful, arrogant "giant" of Communism would lie slain as the powerful, polished "stone" of God's purposes finally lodged in his temple. That time has come.

In 1991, the first evangelistic crusade was held in the stadium of the capital city, Tirana. A number of the converts were baptized in water, openly declaring their allegiance to the Lord Jesus. The Church in Albania was birthed. When Jim and I went to Albania in 1992, there were fifteen church fellowships. At one of them, I spoke to two hundred people, comprising new converts and others who were inquirers of Christianity. Albania now has over one hundred church fellowships.

Since then, several discipleship training schools have been conducted by YWAM in Tirana, in association with Von Golder, an American missionary doing a unique pioneering work in this country. I received a letter about the students from my friend Reona Joly who taught in one of those schools:

> Their hunger for God and His Word, their zeal to communicate the reality of their faith to their countrymen, their hope for the future, can only be explained by the fact that God has answered the prayers of His Church worldwide.

One of the first converts is now leading a discipleship training school.

Many other vital Christian organizations are demonstrating the reality and practicality of God and His kingdom throughout Albania in areas such as:

- the evangelization and discipleship of individuals and the development of the national church;
- biblically based reformation of Albanian society and culture;
- the natural environment.

Many missionaries have a vision for Albania to become a gateway for the spreading of the gospel among other nations. A number of Albanians have already been on short-term missions to other nations, and several have responded to a long-term missionary call. It is also thrilling to know that Albanian Christians are developing in spiritual leadership.

The ongoing prayers of God's people for the young Church in Albania are *crucial* at this time in its history. At the time of completing this book in 1997, a violent uprising against the Albanian Government has been taking place among the general population. In the midst of much fear, shooting, looting, and food shortages, the fledgling church in Albania is remaining strong in the strength of the Lord, alone. One missionary has written saying he is privy to stories "of some of the heroics of simple Believers who are winning the fight to cling to the Lord in the face of death, serious beatings, regular death threats, close brushes with rape, and rampant robbery at gun point. In the midst of this kind of fire, God's faithfulness hasn't even blinked. Those who have managed to face these trials and haven't lost the battle with our enemy fear, have found a new authority in Jesus' name that they've never known before."

The nations of Senegal, Bhutan, Chad, and Azerbaijan are currently among the most resistant to the gospel. When we make them special intercessory prayer targets, they too, like Albania, will crack and split open to the flood tide of God's redemptive purposes.

SUGGESTED PRAYER

Hallelujah, Lord! Your truth is surely marching on. Better yet, You Who are Truth, as the Commander-in-Chief, lead the indomitable army of the Church universal—triumphant and victorious because of Your shed blood.

What a tremendous privilege to be alive at this time in history. Don't let me miss a single purpose related to that privilege.

As always, I'm impressed with Who You are and how You operate, so I bow my head and bend my knees and worship You with awe and wonder.

I commit to responding to Satan's challenge to Your people by believing You for more breakthroughs in relation to the extension of Your kingdom as I intercede for nations most resistant to the gospel. Amen.

14

Spiritual Warfare

The Christian life is an adventure in warfare (Ephesians 6:12; 2 Corinthians 10:3–4). Since a basic strategy of warfare is to know the strengths and weaknesses of both sides, it is imperative that we understand the strength of our Commander-in-Chief as well as the strengths and weaknesses of the enemy. Failure to keep these two factors in perspective will cause distortions in our thoughts, prayers, and actions.

Thousands of years ago, Moses, as chairman of the Israelites' joint chiefs of staff, asked the vital question: Who is our Supreme Commander? The answer pierced the air with crystal clarity; "I AM WHO I AM." (Exodus 3:14). Electric! Fascinating! Authoritative! All-encompassing! Conclusive! God is:

- supreme in authority
- timeless in existence
- unquestionable in sovereignty
- ingenious in creativity
- limitless in power
- terrible in wrath
- majestic in splendor
- awesome in holiness
- infinite in wisdom and knowledge

- ✿ unsearchable in understanding
- ✿ dazzling in beauty
- ✿ unfathomable in love
- ✿ incomprehensible in humility
- ✿ absolute in justice
- ✿ unending in mercy
- ✿ matchless in grace

God has totality of ownership, and is the ruling, reigning Monarch of the universe with an indestructible, eternal kingdom. I'm impressed with, and therefore excited about God, King God, before whom every knee shall bow and every tongue confess that His Son is Lord of all.

I can understand the psalmist's unabashed enthusiasm when he invites us to join him in appropriate expressions of praise and worship to God:

"Clap your hands, all you nations; shout to God with cries of joy. How awesome is the LORD Most High, the great King over all the earth! Sing praises to God, sing praises; sing praises to our King, sing praises. For God is the King of all the earth; sing to him a psalm of praise. God reigns over the nations; God is seated on his holy throne"(Psalm 47:1–2; 6–8).

This Almighty Being lives within me. That's enough to keep me clapping, singing, shouting, laughing, whistling, skipping, jumping, dancing, cartwheeling, and just plain ol' rejoicing, from here on through eternity. Hallelujah!

Knowing who our Commander-in-Chief is, we now ask who our enemy is. Our enemy is nothing more than a fallen angel doomed to eternal destruction (Isaiah 14:12; Revelation 20:10).

I refuse to be impressed with that status. God obviously isn't. If we fear the devil, we have become impressed with him.

Let's not overestimate Satan's abilities. He has no ability to create, so Satan uses the same old tactics he's used since Genesis. God's Word says that we're to fear only the One who has the authority to determine our eternal destiny (Luke 12:5). Oh, the insanity of pride that would cause a person to oppose our Captain and think that he or she could win! The hard fact is that Satan does! Such pride is not only obnoxious, it's ludicrous.

Even so, Satan and his emissaries are never allowed to do anything to a child of God other than what God permits for our ultimate good. The story of Job highlights this truth (Job 42). God is committed to bringing only blessing to everyone submitted to His Lordship.

The forces of darkness are neither omnipotent, omniscient, nor omnipresent. That is why they cannot be the cause of every Christian's problems. To think and speak otherwise is to deify the enemy. God forbid! We should never recount a story of what we believe is satanic activity among Christians without either a corresponding story of Satan's total defeat, or our certain belief that when God's purposes are accomplished, the enemy will be defeated.

So as not to underestimate the enemy, we need to know what the Bible says about him. Three times in the gospel of John (12:31; 14:30; 16:11) the Lord Jesus refers to him as "the prince of this world." The following Scriptures are related to Satan's limited power: "...the whole world is under the control of the evil one" (1 John 5:19b). "...now the prince of this world will be driven out" (John 12:31b). "The god of this age [Satan] has blinded the minds of unbelievers..." (2 Corinthians 4:4a) "Be self-controlled and alert. Your enemy the devil prowls around like a roaring lion looking for someone to devour. Resist him, standing firm in the faith..." (I Peter 5:8–9a).

A look at the numerical strengths of both God's army and Satan's army is interesting. Satan has a minority of fallen angels known as demons, with limited power, plus the majority of people. These forces are opposing the triune God and the majority of angelic hosts, who have unlimited power, and the minority of people, who have God's power. Romans 8:31b gives us the right perspective on these statistics: "If God is for us, who can be against us?" Therefore, one believer and God is always a vast majority.

The Bible says that Satan *walks* up and down on the earth, going to and fro. It also says, "...the eyes of the Lord run to and *fro throughout the whole earth, to show his might in behalf of those whose heart is blameless toward him"* [emphasis added] (2 Chronicles 16:9a RSV). God's eyes are ahead of Satan's feet every time. God is always looking for someone who will listen to Him, believe Him, and obey Him, so that He can demonstrate His power to them and through them.

A small YWAM team, mostly from Brazil, listened to God and were called by Him to go to India. God revealed to the team while in prayer that His strategy to reach the lost was to first have a year of intercession with regular times of fasting as part of the needed spiritual warfare to break the enemy's strongholds. The team obeyed.

God then directed them to focus their evangelistic efforts on the people of Goa, who were unevangelized. Among the 80,000 people scattered in more than 100 villages, there was not one Goan believer. As a result of the team's intensive preparation, God broke through in might and power. It became routine to hold their outreaches inside the Hindu temples. Sometimes, because of overflow crowds, everyone moves out to the temple courtyards.

The Goa people are very open to the gospel and are responding to its message. The missionaries are calling out for more laborers to be sent into this ripened harvest field. They plan to establish a mission center in Goa to train and send laborers to other parts of India and surrounding nations.

PREPARATION FOR COMBAT

Our ultimate resource for knowledge on this subject must be the Word of God and our application of it. *"I write to you, young men, because you are strong, and the word of God lives in you, and you have overcome the evil one"* (1 John 2:14b).

1.   Keep our focus on the supreme authority of the Lord Jesus Christ as Captain of the Lord of hosts.

"All authority in heaven and on earth has been given to me" (Matthew 28:18b).

2.   See the enemy in light of God's greatness, Jesus' victory over him at the cross, and his ultimate defeat.

"The reason the Son of God appeared was to destroy the devil's work" (1 John 3:8b).

3. Exercise worship and praise.

Not only does this keep our focus in the right direction, but the Bible teaches that power over the enemy is released by God through praise (2 Chronicles 20:22; Psalm 149:5–9). I love the way Dr. Jack Hayford puts it in his book *Worship His Majesty*;[1] "Worship has the power to neutralize the power of demonic attack upon the people of God, for wherever the spirit of praise resides, God is enthroned and neither flesh nor devil can successfully perpetuate their designs."

4. Humble ourselves before God.

We need to declare that we are totally unimpressed with ourselves, and that our only strength is in Him. Since the enemy's character is based in pride, we can overcome the enemy only through humility. Verbally agree with God: *"...apart from me you can do nothing"* (John 15:5b); *"You are my Lord; apart from you I have no good thing'"* (Psalm 16:2b).

My husband and I were part of a group of five spiritual leaders who were called by God on one occasion to confront a false prophet. Although we had been with the man for hours, we had felt no release from the Holy Spirit to carry out the purpose for which we had gathered. Then one of the leaders openly confessed and repented of spiritual pride. Immediately that leader was released with authority to confront the man.

5. Make sure we have no unrepented sin in our lives.

Jesus said, *"...the ruler of this world is coming, and he has nothing in Me"* (John 14:30b NKJV). The Revised Standard Version's wording is *"He has no power over me."* Jesus could proclaim this because He was walking in the light with no areas of darkness in His life. Walking in the light of the Lord is powerful protection against the enemy. *"So let us put aside the deeds of darkness and put on the armor of light"* (Romans 13:12b).

---

1. by Word Books, 1987

Where there is continued harassment from the enemy in any area of our lives, we need to ask God to reveal whether we have created a platform for the enemy to work on us. Unrepented sin can be the cause. Ephesians 4:27 warns us not to give the devil a foothold. The previous two verses refer to the sins of any form of deceit or anger with a bitter spirit.

God initially allowed Job's onslaughts from the enemy as a test to Job's reaction to adversity. In the case of Daniel, the enemy interference in Daniel chapter 10 was part of an intensive spiritual battle in the heavenlies. The diligent seeker of truth will be rewarded with an accurate understanding of the cause of, or purpose for, the enemy's activity.

6. Fulfill the conditions to be empowered by the Holy Spirit.

Jesus, as Son of Man, was empowered by the Holy Spirit at his baptism (Luke 3:21–22) before his confrontation with Satan in the wilderness. *"Jesus, full of the Holy Spirit, returned from the Jordan and was led by the Spirit in the desert, where for forty days he was tempted by the devil"* (Luke 4:1–2a).

God the Holy Spirit wants to completely control our lives so that the Lord Jesus Christ may be made more real to us, and then through us to others. Without His control we will be powerless to live the Christian life, and ineffective in our witness to others. Paul tells us to *"...be strong in the Lord and in his mighty power"* (Ephesians 6:10). This is possible only to the degree we are empowered by the Holy Spirit as we are commanded in Ephesians 5:18. Such empowerment is made possible by constantly fulfilling the following conditions.

    a. Surrender your will totally to God, *"...the Holy Spirit, whom God has given to those who obey him"* (Acts 5:32b).

    b. Be thorough in confession and repentance of all known sin. *"He who conceals his sins does not prosper, but whoever confesses and renounces them finds mercy"* (Proverbs 28:13).

    c. Ask God to fill you with His Spirit. *"If you then, though you are evil, know how to give good gifts to your children, how much more will your Father in heaven give the Holy Spirit to those who ask him!"* (Luke 11:13).

d. Believe that He will, and thank Him for doing so *"...everything that does not come from faith is sin"* (Romans 14:23b).

e. Allow the Holy Spirit to manifest Himself in whichever way He chooses by being obedient to His promptings.

7. Realize the necessity of being in unity with all other believers.

"Every kingdom divided against itself will be ruined, and every city or household divided against itself will not stand" (Matthew 12:25b).

We're only as strong against the frequent bombing raids and artillery fire of our enemy as he tries to wound and destroy the Body of Christ, as we are united. Biblical unity is impenetrable, indomitable strength. Satan is no match for it (Psalm 133:1–3).

8. "...put on the full armor of God..." (Ephesians 6:13) piece-by-piece by faith.

"...clothe yourselves with the Lord Jesus Christ" (Romans 13:14a). His life represents the armor:

- The helmet of salvation. *"He alone is my rock and my salvation..."* (Psalm 62:2a).
- The breastplate of righteousness. *"...Christ Jesus is made unto us wisdom, and righteousness"* (1 Corinthians 1:30b KJV).
- The girdle of truth. *"I am the...truth"* (John 14:6b).
- The shield of faith. *"...I live by the faith of the Son of God"* (Galatians 2:20b KJV).
- The gospel of peace. *"For he himself is our peace"* (Ephesians 2:14a).
- The sword of the Spirit which is the Word of God. *"The Word became flesh..."* (John 1:14a).

We cannot put on the armor if it doesn't fit. We cannot put on truth if we have unconfessed lies in our life; we cannot put on righteousness if we are aware of unrighteousness in our life.

9. Declare by faith

a. Our position: *"And God raised us up with Christ and seated us with him in the heavenly realms in Christ Jesus"* (Ephesians 2:6).

b. Our protection: *"The name of the* LORD *is a strong tower; the righteous run to it and are safe"* (Proverbs 18:10).

Be on the offensive, not the defensive. Satanic forces get away with only as much as the Body of Christ allows them. David didn't wait until Goliath attacked him. He ran toward the giant, taking the initiative in warfare. He started and ended the skirmish. Likewise, we can take our God-given authority over the enemy and have him running before he has a chance to assault us.

SUGGESTED PRAYER

I bow before You, God, in humble adoration and sing,
"Majesty, worship His Majesty!
Unto Jesus, be all glory, honor and praise.
Majesty, Kingdom authority,
Flows from His throne, unto His own,
His anthem raise.
So exalt, lift up on high the name of Jesus,
Magnify, come glorify Christ Jesus the King.
Majesty, worship His Majesty
Jesus who died, now glorified,
King of all kings."[1]
Amen.

---

2. "Majesty." Words and music by Jack Hayford. Rocksmith Music ASCAP, all rights reserved. Used by permission.

┌─────┐
│ **15** │
└─────┘

Avoiding Hindrances
to Intercession

WAITING ON GOD

It was in Alexandria, Egypt, about twenty minutes before we were due to leave for a Thursday morning session of a spiritual leadership conference. Loren Cunningham, founder and International Chairman of YWAM; Don Stephens, now president of YWAM's International Mercy Ships, and I were the speakers.

We had met as usual, before each session, for prayer. It came time to pray for Loren as he was to be the speaker that morning. I was waiting on God for the Holy Spirit's direction to know how to most effectively intercede for him. No impressions came so I continued to wait. Still nothing. The others had prayed, so I explained that I hadn't as yet heard the Holy Spirit's direction.

Joseph Farragala, our YWAM leader for Egypt and our interpreter, arrived to take Loren and Don to the conference center. I stayed behind to prepare for speaking at the afternoon session.

We were all aware that because of the difficulties in parking outside the building in which we were being housed, Joseph was concerned about leaving his car for more than a few minutes. I finally told Loren that I understood perfectly if

149

he felt he should leave. I left the decision with him. He said, "I'll wait." (Loren has a track record for making room for God, which I deeply appreciate.)

I kept on waiting, as I had done on numerous other occasions in my life, encouraging myself from God's Word. *"those who wait for me shall not be put to shame"* (Isaiah 49:23b RSV).

After this testing period, God broke through, but not with a prayer. A message was impressed upon my mind to give to Loren. "I am going to bring a leader across your path today. Watch for him and do not miss my purposes. They are important." I spoke the words and worshiped God for His faithfulness. None of us had the faintest idea what the message meant. The three men left and I, like they, went about our Father's business.

Loren was sensitively alert to every person with whom he had a conversation that day. But the fulfillment of the word from the Lord didn't come that way. Instead, in the late afternoon, Joseph received a phone call from Cairo from one of two men who were attendees at the first two days of the conference. They had reported back to their spiritual leader in Cairo, Father Zachariah. He in turn felt impressed to ask us three speakers and Joseph to visit him on Friday evening at his headquarters before we had to go to the airport for our flight departures.

We knew nothing about this man, but as we sought God, the Holy Spirit gave us the assurance that we were to make the effort. We did. What a reward awaited us! What an historically significant meeting! What a precious, vital leader to the Egyptian people we found!

What a powerful, effective ministry Father Zachariah had in training leaders, making disciples, and evangelizing, with signs following the preaching of the Word of God as in the book of Acts. Our hearts were bonded together in love and unity as we listened, shared, and prayed together about the things of God.

I felt a strong call from the Lord to pray fervently and regularly for this man of God, and did so for years. It came as a shock a few years later to hear that Father Zachariah had been imprisoned for his faith under President Anwar Sadat's leadership. The link in intercession was only strengthened, as Father Zachariah was incarcerated for years.

God assured me that the unexpected meeting in Cairo was the fulfillment of the word of the Lord. I praised God for confirming to me again that waiting on Him in prayer brings forth His maximum purposes.

The more we yield to the Holy Spirit when in prayer for others, the more we'll discover how intriguing God is. We really never know what He's going to do next. One thing is certain—there's never a dull moment when we're receiving orders from "Headquarters Heaven." The variety of God's ways never ceases to amaze and fascinate me.

We experience the adventure of intercession to the degree we have learned to wait on God. Everything about our human nature rebels against waiting. To those of us who were born in "overdrive," waiting is not our favorite pastime. We could identify with the people in Isaiah's day to whom the prophet said, *"Woe...to those who say, 'Let God hurry, let him hasten his work so we may see it. Let it approach'"* (Isaiah 5:18–19a). However, we discover that waiting on God in humility and faith because of Who He is, and obeying His signals according to His timetable, are really where the exciting action is.

Waiting is a discipline that has tremendous rewards. And yet vast numbers of Christians, including many who pray for others, seldom, if ever make it a way of life.

Why? Because of ignorance, impatience, or failure to study from God's Word the character of the One Who calls them to wait. The reward for those who diligently seek to know God is God's revelation of Himself, and that produces motivation to wait on Him. Our prayer life is only as powerful as our knowledge of the character of God—every single fascinating facet of it. David had this thirst for and subsequent knowledge of God (Psalm 63:1–2). That's why David could say, *"My soul, wait silently for God alone, for my expectation is from Him"* (Psalm 62:5 NKJV).

We need to stop and think about how God in His humility has waited for us to have the humility to wait on Him!

NO PRESUMPTION

Presumption about the most effective way to intercede for others not only hinders maximum effectiveness but causes us to miss the thrilling sense of adventure God wants to bless us with in this wonderful ministry.

How do we know with our finite minds whether God wants to move through us with weeping, travailing, wrestling, fasting, the gifts of the Holy Spirit, dreams, visions, mental pictures, impressions, verses of Scripture quickened to us, or silence? So often we don't—until we've waited on God and given Him time to move on and through us. And when God does move, we must never presume that He's going to do it the same way the next time. While the Holy Spirit is unpredictable in His movements, He is totally dependable in His character. He can direct us to do unusual things that bypass our human reasoning, but God will not direct us to take actions against His character or that contradict His Word, the Bible.

If and when the Holy Spirit moves upon us in group intercession in some of the more unusual vocal ways previously listed, there will usually be a witness in the spirit of the leadership that this is of God. If we're in doubt, we can always quietly submit our impressions to the spiritual leadership first.

It is very important that we do not quench the Holy Spirit through disobedience (1 Thessalonians 5:19). It is equally important that we do not grieve the Holy Spirit and become a stumbling block to others by not exercising the fruit of the spirit of self-control when needed. Remember, *"The spirits of prophets are subject to the control of prophets. For God is not a God of disorder but of peace"* (1 Corinthians 14:32–33a).

FEAR OF THE LORD

How can we know the constraint of the Holy Spirit and the restraint in each situation—especially when they're related to the unusual? To the degree we are controlled by the fear of the

Lord. *"The fear of the* LORD *is the beginning of wisdom; all who follow his precepts have good understanding"* (Psalm 111:10a).

I have written a book titled, *Intimate Friendship with God—Through Understanding the Fear of the Lord.*[1] It explains how this subject affects every aspect of our lives. When the truths are applied, godly wisdom and behavior follow. God will always honor the humility and faith of every heart that depends upon the truth. *"Likewise the Spirit helps us in our weakness; for we do not know how to pray as we ought..."* (Romans 8:26a RSV). He helps us to know what to do to please Him at all times.

We can become so cautious in group praying that we miss God's purposes, usually because of the fear of men. I received the following letter that illustrates this from a woman of God who is an intercessor:

Dear Joy,

I just wanted to share a result of a message you gave at a Spiritual Leadership Conference in Northern California. In one of your illustrations you said God told you to lie on your face on the floor when speaking to a group of spiritual leaders and that you instantly obeyed, resulting in a deep move of God's Spirit among them.

That hit me hard as I was disobedient in obeying a similar prompting but in a different setting.

Our new church facility was being built and the intercessory prayer group was meeting on Monday evening in the entry hall area. The Lord told me to get up off my knees, lie in front of the main entrance and pray that a spirit of repentance would fall on all who enter and that no unclean spirit would dwell in the building. I disobeyed God. That was nearly five years ago.

---

1. by Chosen Books, Revell, 1986

At the end of your message I confessed this to a pastor who was seated behind me in the service. At the following Monday church prayer meeting, I openly confessed my disobedience, then took my place on my face before the front doors of our church and prayed the above prayer. By God's grace and mercy, the next week to the day, two women in leadership each confessed before our Deacon Board the sin of adultery—one had covered up for five years and the other for nine years.

As a result of these sins being exposed, two pastors on our church staff have resigned.

I am awed at the hand of God being manifest after such delayed obedience on my part.

This story is a reminder that we must never minimize the repercussions of our simple steps of obedience to the Holy Spirit's promptings.

SUGGESTED PRAYER

Faithful God,

Thank You for the reminder that "Since ancient times no one has heard, no ear has perceived, no eye has seen any God besides you, who acts on behalf of those who wait for him" (Isaiah 64:4).

Teach me the discipline and subsequent rewards of waiting on You as a way of life. Keep me from presumption when praying for others, and teach me the ways of the Spirit. May the fear of the Lord so permeate my being that I will always be motivated to obey You solely because of Who You are.

Thank You that You will work these graces in me as I believe You and obey You. I trust You and love You.

Amen.

16

Diversity of God's Ways in Intercession

WORSHIPING AND PRAISING GOD

Worship is our highest service. Everything we do for God should start with worship, lead us to more worship, and culminate in worship. Vocal praise is an outcome of a life of worship. *"I will extol the LORD at all times; his praise will always be on my lips"* (Psalm 34:1).

Intercession should start with praise, be interspersed with praise, and end with praise. This keeps the focus where it should be—on God Himself. No matter how big the problem or how much we pray about it, vocal praise to God reminds us that He is the ultimate source and solution. This stimulates faith and motivates us to give Him all the glory, regardless of how much He uses us. *"My whole being will exclaim, 'Who is like you, O LORD?'"* (Psalm 35:10a).

God has chosen praise and worship as a climate for releasing His power. God is honored, and we are exposed to His dynamic action. *"Let everything that has breath praise the Lord"* (Psalm 150:6a).

MEDITATING ON SCRIPTURE

Meditating on the Scriptures under the Holy Spirit's enabling is a powerful means of inspiring us to have a closer

155

relationship with the Lord Jesus. After all, Jesus is the Living Word. Meditation takes us to greater heights and deeper levels of intercession. It is also a tremendous faith booster. *"So then faith comes by hearing, and hearing by the word of God"* (Romans 10:17 NKJV).

Try the following Scripture for starters. It never ceases to exhilarate me.

"David praised the LORD in the presence of the whole assembly, saying, 'Praise be to you, O LORD, God of our father Israel, from everlasting to everlasting. Yours, O LORD, is the greatness and the power and the glory and the majesty and the splendor, for everything in heaven and earth is yours. Yours, O LORD, is the kingdom; you are exalted as head over all. Wealth and honor come from you; you are the ruler of all things. In your hands are strength and power to exalt and give strength to all. Now, our God, we give you thanks, and praise your glorious name'" (1 Chronicles 29:10–13).

Memorization of Scripture is important, and has powerful potential to effect change in our lives. We cannot guarantee that we will always have access to a Bible, since adverse circumstances or an inability to read one for any of a number of reasons can occur. But once we have the Bible embedded in our memory, the Holy Spirit uses this to powerfully minister to us in times of need. However, *meditation* is of even more value than *memorization* because meditation encourages *revelation*. And revelation of truth is the mostpowerful factor to motivate us to make *application*. Only then can the truth set us free.

In group praying, the leader can seek God ahead of time for direction as to which part of God's Word the people need to meditate on. It is very helpful for prayer groups to have teaching on meditation. (I recommend that the reader obtain the Lydia Fellowship's materials that are available on this subject. The USA address is P.O. Box 20236, San Jose, CA 95160.)

It is always advantageous to have the Scriptures with us when we're praying or likely to be praying for others. We should be alert and listening to the Holy Spirit in case He wants to give us direction, instruction, exhortation, encouragement, or confirmation from God's Word. Often He does. This is a thrilling and fulfilling part of the ministry of intercession, and has become a way of life for me for decades. The frequency of these experiences never ceases to leave me in awe of God and His ways, and motivates me to worship Him.

RELEASING THE WEIGHT

God burdens our spirit about a person or a situation so that we may cast that burden upon the Lord (Psalm 55:22).

We are not meant to go around with a heavy heart and a weight on our spirit. The cure is to simply invite the Holy Spirit to direct and energize us as we take prayer action about the situation. Start praying what God gives, and release faith with every request. We'll know when we have moved from hoping to believing. The burden will be lifted from our spirit. As we continue praising God that He's working, we'll find His yoke is easy and His burden is light.

PRAYING IN THE SPIRIT

Any prayer that originates from the Holy Spirit and is directed, energized, and sustained by Him qualifies as a prayer that is prayed in the Spirit. It falls into the same category as being in the Spirit, talking in the Spirit, and singing in the Spirit. For example, the apostle John tells us that he was "in the Spirit on the Lord's day" when he heard and saw visions of God (Revelation 1:10–11).

Praying in the Spirit simply means that we've fulfilled the conditions to be controlled by the Holy Spirit in prayer. Paul urges us to this kind of praying in the context of spiritual warfare. *"And pray in the Spirit on all occasions with all kinds of prayers and requests. With this in mind, be alert and always keep on praying for all the saints"* (Ephesians 6:18). Jude also exhorts us to build ourselves up in our most holy faith and pray in the Holy Spirit (verse 20). The context is related to a call to persevere in times of opposition, making sure we're manifesting God's love at all times.

CHARACTERISTICS OF PRAYERS DIRECTED BY THE HOLY SPIRIT

Prayers directed by the Holy Spirit
- will be according to God's will (1 John 5:14–15)).
- will glorify the Father through the Son (John 14:13).
- are based upon God's character, ways, and Word (John 15:7).
- come from a clean heart (James 5:16).
- are prayed in full assurance of faith (James 1:6)
- are asked in Jesus' name (John 14:14).

They always get answered!

I am indebted to my dear friend Arthur Wallis, for pointing out the difference between praying in the Spirit (capital "S") and praying with the spirit (small "s") in chapter 3 of his excellent book *Pray in the Spirit*.[1] Arthur Wallis was a renowned author and Bible teacher who went to be with the Lord some years ago.

PRAYING WITH THE SPIRIT (SMALL "s")

When the phrase "praying with the spirit" is used, all Bible translations use a small "s." This form of praying occurs when a person has been graced by the Holy Spirit with another language that he or she has never learned (glossolalia). It is a means of praising God beyond the limits of one's finite mind (1 Corinthians 14:2). It is also a means for the Holy Spirit to intercede through us when God sees that it is wiser for us or others not to know the prayer's content. The Bible says that we are personally edified by exercising this working of Holy Spirit grace in our lives (1 Corinthians 14:4).

Over a lifetime, I have participated in prayer meetings where praying in the Spirit and praying with the spirit were evidenced. Among godly, seasoned intercessors there were some who prayed in another language that God had given them, and some who didn't. One was not necessarily more powerful or

---

1. England: Kingsway Publications, 1970

more effective than another. This should not be surprising; in both categories, the people praying were fulfilling the same conditions. They were all submitted to the Holy Spirit's control, were obeying His promptings, and had been empowered by the Holy Spirit as commanded in Ephesians 5:18.

Another excellent book I would recommend is *The Beauty of Spiritual Language*[2] by Dr. Jack Hayford.

TEARS AND TRAVAIL

When the burden in prayer is intensified to where words are inadequate, the Holy Spirit expresses the Father's heart toward the object of the prayer in a travail of involuntary, regular groaning similar to sounds a woman makes just before the birth of a child. The physical pain is replaced by an intensity of desire, coupled with faith that God is birthing something very significant in the spiritual realm. I have experienced this on many occasions when praying for individual spiritual leaders. At times the Holy Spirit has given me immediate understanding as to the cause and purpose of the travail. At other times, He has withheld all understanding until considerably later.

The spiritual development of a man or woman of God is a lengthy process. So although results were not immediately apparent, I have been confident that God was working something deep and permanent in their lives.

The same principle applies to revival praying. It has been a great encouragement to me for four decades of praying for revival for the nations, including this kind of travail, that God has promised that the labor will not be in vain.

" *'Who has ever heard of such a thing? Who has ever seen such things? Can a country be born in a day or a nation be brought forth in a moment? Yet no sooner is Zion in labor than she gives birth to her children. Do I bring to the moment of birth and not give delivery?' "says the* LORD. *'Do I close up the womb when I bring to delivery?' says your God"* (Isaiah 66:8–9).

---

2. Dallas Texas: Word Publishing, 1992

Desperate desire expressed in intense weeping is another way the Holy Spirit manifests God's heart in intercession. This has happened to me numerous times in praying for nations, missionary organizations, churches, spiritual leaders, people groups, individuals, and lost souls.

It is significant that this depth of praying preceded my being called of God to be involved with reaching needy people groups. It is the greatest preparation we can have.

Many years ago, Arthur Wallis asked me to write anonymously about my experiences of tears and travail in intercession. He included my account in his book *Pray in the Spirit*.[3] While it was right at that time that the chapter be written anonymously, I believe it is equally right to lift that veil now.

When Peter, James, and John came down from the Mount of Transfiguration, Jesus gave them strict instructions not to tell anyone at that time what they had seen (Matthew 17:9). But at a later time, Matthew, Mark, and Luke were moved upon by the Holy Spirit to write about the event, obviously having had it related to them by the three disciples who were there.

God was glorified by these acts of obedience. He has assured me that the same principle applies in relation to my sharing many things in this book that have previously been untold. I have not arrived at this conclusion quickly or easily.

Following are two experiences that I previously shared in the book *Pray in the Spirit*.

After a day of prayer and fasting for souls to be saved prior to a Billy Graham Crusade, this intense weeping came upon me as I prayed for a Jew, very influential in both religious and business circles. I had already prayed for him for two years. He came with us

---

3. England: Kingsway Publications, 1970

to the Crusade and was deeply stirred by the Holy Spirit. This was followed by a further year of intercession, after which he died suddenly, without our knowing whether or not he had found Christ. God alone knows the destiny of this man's soul. I learned much through this experience, of God's pursuing love (p.101).

I also learned that no prayers that have originated from God and have been prayed back to Him in faith are ever wasted. Even if the purposes were not fulfilled in the object of our prayers, divine purpose has been worked out in us.

The other experience related to an intense agony for a lost soul. It was experienced in circumstances that made it inexpedient for any groanings to be expressed at all.

One Sunday morning the preacher announced that he would be preaching that night on the subject of hell from the story of the rich man and Lazarus, and that there might be someone in the evening service for whom it would be the last opportunity to receive Christ. He asked for special prayer. I knew at once that this referred to an unconverted friend, a business executive, with whom my husband had faithfully shared the way of salvation on several occasions, and for whom much prayer had been made. We phoned him and he consented to come. In the afternoon as I prayed, the burden of his desperate need came upon me, and words gave way to intense weeping with a great longing that he would repent before it was too late.

That evening he sat beside us throughout the service as the Holy Spirit agonized through me for his salvation. In utter silence and perfect stillness of body I experienced a travail of spirit as intense as anything I had ever known. It seemed I could see his soul spiralling down to a lost eternity, and, as I prayed without ceasing, I sensed the force of the Holy Spirit's work was gradually but surely drawing the man back. The only outward indication that anything was happening to me, was the silent falling of tears. He responded to the appeal, and after the service he knelt with the preacher, repented of his sin and committed his life to Christ (p. 101).

Oh the depth of God's pursuing love and unending mercy. I pause, and worship Him.

The most intense travail I have ever experienced in intercession for those in leadership was when two men with whom I have been closely associated for many years were having a conversation. I knew they were having relational problems and were trying to solve them. Because I had more knowledge than most others had of their difficulties, I felt very responsible to be in fervent intercession for them at that time.

Withdrawing to a secluded place where I could be completely private and undisturbed, I gave myself to God in prayer on behalf of both men. I was aware that each one had experienced pain in this relationship, and my heart was full of compassion for them both as I felt some of their pain. The burden in my spirit for them to come to unity and healing was intense. I longed for the Spirit's travail to come upon me as a mother longs for the labor pains that bring forth a child. Groans and tears did not come—but rather, short, gasping, panting breaths and grunts with an indescribable agony of spirit.

I inquired of God. "What is *this*?" His response was that He was sharing His pure, impartial love for both men equally with my heart. Understanding came that I was experiencing some of *His* pain that came from this quality of love for them both. While I was relieved when the burden lifted, I was grateful to have experienced at a deeper level how God yearns for His children to be in unity and how He suffers until they are. In time, unity and healing came to these precious men of God.

SUGGESTED PRAYER

Dear God,

I worship You and praise Your wonderful name for the diversity and wisdom of Your ways. Thank You for revealing them to Your children.

I long to experience them more fully in intercession so that I can better understand You and Your great, big, compassionate heart.

Thank You that the Holy Spirit will be my teacher. I love You, God. Amen.

17

Are You Prepared?

One of our greatest needs is to have a far greater revelation of God's character, His glory, and His manifest presence. Nothing produces that more effectively than when the Holy Spirit is poured out in revival power upon God's people. Are we prepared for our great need to be met?

Genuine revival is truly awesome. God comes down with an unusually strong sense of His presence, so often manifesting His indescribable holiness first. Sin is seen from God's perspective, and His children have the opportunity to repent under those conditions. Just one of God's ways in evidencing His great heart of love to us.

Releases of exultant joy and praise are experienced by those who cooperate with the rain of the Holy Spirit. We can choose to either put up our umbrellas of resistance or invite God to soak us.

An amplified awareness of the white-hot holiness of our intensely loving, vibrantly real, spectacularly powerful Lord will do more to motivate us to live for eternal issues than anything else I know. That's what we desperately need. That's what revival brings!

Our hearts need to be prepared by the Holy Spirit for the awesome outpouring of the fire, wind, and rain of the Spirit that is coming. It won't be a picnic. As someone has said, "When we pray for rain, we need to be prepared to deal with some mud." God ploughs deeply in the hearts of those who *want* to be prepared. Let us not flinch at the pain of the blades, but look forward to the display of His glory and the mighty harvest that will result to the praise of His glory.

Revival produces the strongest evidence of the life of the Lord Jesus Christ in every believer. When God's people are truly revived, Jesus Christ Himself becomes their greatest passion for living. The light of the world then glows and shows! The spillover to the unconverted world is remarkable. A great spiritual awakening takes place, and multitudes of hardened sinners not normally affected by the gospel deeply repent of their sin and commit their lives to Christ.

Whole communities are inevitably affected by this spiritual phenomenon, and history proves that social reform follows. God at work in human lives becomes the focal point of the daily news. Imagine that! What a welcome change from the stream of reports of rape and murder and other forms of violence.

In real revival, God does more to extend His kingdom in seconds and minutes than would normally be accomplished in days, weeks, months, or years of God-inspired and energized Christian activity. At the height of the 1857–58 spiritual awakening that swept America, it was estimated that 50,000 conversions were occurring weekly—without Christian radio or television broadcasts!

David Brainerd, a mighty intercessor, described how God answered his fervent, persistent prayers for revival among the American Indians in 1745.

> The power of God seemed to descend upon the assembly like a mighty rushing wind, and with an astonishing energy bore down all before it. I stood amazed at the influence which seized the audience almost universally; and would compare it to nothing more than the irresistible force of a mighty torrent. Almost all persons of all ages, including children, were

bowed down and in deep distress over the state of their souls, oblivious of those around them. They were universally praying and crying for mercy in every part of the building and many out of doors.

Genuine revivals produce a revolution of righteousness more quickly, and with greater permanency, than anything else. Because God's Word says, *"Righteousness exalts a nation"* (Proverbs 14:34a), then surely prayer for revival is of paramount importance. I'm convinced it's revival for survival.

Our world is in such a shocking state, and our society is so sick, that if it weren't for the fact that I know that God wants to bring genuine revival to His Church in every nation and accompanying reformation, I would be in despair. But I'm not in despair. I have expectant hope and firm faith, because *revival praying moves the hand of God.*

Before we get into that subject, I'm convinced we need to understand how essential biblical unity is. In fact, the effectiveness of our prayers for revival is dependent upon it.

Jesus said that the one thing that would convince the world that God sent His Son into the world and that God loves His disciples as He loves His Son would be true unity among His people. Such unity is characterized by how the three persons of the Trinity relate to each other: *"I in them and you in me. May they be brought to complete unity to let the world know that you sent me and have loved them even as you have loved me"* (John 17:23).

As soon as Jesus prayed that prayer, the Father started to answer it. It is therefore possible to experience this unique unity with the Holy Spirit's enabling.

This quality of unity among all of God's people is essentially linked with a major harvest of lost souls. It was so with the early Church. Three things set the stage for the outpouring of the Holy Spirit recorded in Acts chapter 2, resulting in 3,000 souls being converted and baptized in one day.

The conditions were: The preaching of the Word of the Lord with authority, persistent prayer, and unity.

While the importance of anointed preaching is unquestionable, I believe we have over-emphasized this factor to the neglect of the other necessary conditions. And while prevailing prayer is an essential prerequisite to revival, we need to understand that a lot of praying doesn't necessarily impress God at all. It's the attitude of our heart and our lifestyle behind the words that gets His attention. In fact, the Bible tells us that our prayers can actually make God angry and repulse Him: "*O Lord God Almighty, how long will your anger smolder against the prayers of your people?*" (Psalm 80:4). It is very significant that this verse comes in the middle of the psalmist's repeated cries for God to restore and revive His people.

The Bible also says that if we refuse to read and heed God's Word, our prayers are equally distasteful to God. "*If anyone turns a deaf ear to the law, even his prayers are detestable.*" (Proverbs 28:9).

So many times we think (foolishly) that as long as we have enough prayer and preaching, God will send revival. Is it because it takes a lot more time to humble ourselves, forgive one another, and work through misunderstanding in order to be united that we fail to meet one of God's crucial conditions for spiritual awakening?

"*All these with one accord devoted themselves to prayer, together with the women and Mary the mother of Jesus, and with his brothers*" (Acts 1:14 RSV). Who were "all these" who made up the 120? The apostles, together with other men and women disciples, and Jesus' immediate family members. That group hadn't always been in "one accord," reason enough for God's not having previously trusted them with the outpouring of His Spirit.

The original disciples had been competitive and jealous. One had betrayed the Lord; another had denied Him three times. All had been full of unbelief. We are told in John 7:5 that even Jesus' brothers didn't believe in Him. So there had to be a lot of repentance and reconciliation before that group could all come to unity. The fact that they came together and stayed together in one place for about ten days indicates that their unity was deep and real.

To pray effectively for revival, we need to experience unity in the following four ways:

1. Unity of heart with God.

"If I had cherished sin in my heart, the Lord would not have listened" (Psalm 66:18). This means embracing and rejoicing in God's absolute righteousness and justice at all times, regardless of our circumstances.

"He is the Rock, his works are perfect, and all his ways are just. A faithful God who does no wrong, upright and just is he" (Deuteronomy 32:4). It is easy to have hidden resentment against God, especially in times of prolonged trial. Frequently worshiping and praising God as a way of life counteracts that possibility.

2. Unity of heart with all true believers.

We're only as united as we're free from reserves in our hearts. A reserve unchecked will progressively produce coldness, aloofness, resentment, judgment, criticism, lack of confidence, lack of fellowship, lack of love, and disunity. A reserve is less than loving one another deeply from the heart (1 Peter 1:22).

Psalm 15 says that we're only as close to God as we are close in heart to one another. That means our relationship with God is only as close as our relationship with the person to whom we're the coldest in heart.

Is there any section of the Body of Christ with whom we don't want to be identified? Any group or individual believer from whom we feel we have nothing to learn? Any group of believers we wouldn't want to be teamed with in Christian service?

If we can't identify with, learn from, and work with all other Christians now, how can we expect to pray effectively for others and be used by God in revival in the future when everything will be accelerated and the pressures increased? *"If you have raced with men on foot and they have worn you out, how can you compete with horses? If you stumble in safe country, how will you manage in the thickets by the Jordan?"* (Jeremiah 12:5).

3. Unity of purpose.

The main purpose for a revived people is that we may become more conformed to the image of the Lord Jesus (Romans 8:29), and have a greater intimacy of relationship with Him. Another purpose is that multiplied millions may be converted, be set free from their bondages, and become disciples of the Lord Jesus—nurtured by many denominations and Christian organizations.

4. Unity in understanding the ways of the Spirit.

This unity prevents us from resisting the very thing for which we have prayed. In South Africa, on a Sunday evening in a youth meeting of a Dutch Reformed Church, a young black girl working as a farmhand asked that a particular hymn be sung and that she be allowed to pray. After hesitation, her request was granted. While the girl was praying, a noise like approaching thunder was heard in the distance coming closer and closer until it enveloped the hall, shaking the building. The Holy Spirit was then poured out upon the group in new and unusual ways from anything they had experienced. Spontaneously, everyone started to pray loudly and simultaneously.

The youth leader knew it was God and didn't resist the moving of God's Spirit. But the church's pastor, Rev. Andrew Murray, upon arrival at the meeting, tried to stop what he saw happening. He was totally unsuccessful. The same phenomenon occurred at subsequent gatherings, with Andrew Murray again trying to quiet the people. He later repented and cooperated with God, recognizing his need to be open and flexible to new ways of the Spirit's workings. It's a matter of history how God so mightily used him after that. If resisting the Spirit could happen to saintly Andrew Murray in the early days of his pastoral ministry, it could happen to anyone.

We need to constantly cry out to God to teach us His ways:

- Study His ways from His Word.
- Ask for the fear of God to be upon us.

- Constantly submit to the person of the Holy Spirit.
- Obey the Holy Spirit's promptings in everything.

God then imparts spiritual wisdom to discern the varied and wonderful ways of the Spirit's workings.

SPECIAL PRAYER FOR LEADERS

Because all genuine outpourings of the Holy Spirit are characterized by the unusual and unpredictable, we need to pray that God will prepare the spiritual leaders for it.

- Pray that leaders will have understanding of the ways of the Spirit and will make room for God.
- Pray that leaders will be sensitive and flexible to flow with whatever new thing God wants to do.
- Pray that leaders will be taken over by the fear of the Lord and released from the fear of men.
- Pray that leaders will recognize that the fear of the Lord is the source of their much needed wisdom.
- Pray that leaders will be given a deep desire to be radically real, and to repent of all hypocrisy.
- Pray that leaders will not be concerned for their personal reputation.

SUGGESTED PRAYER

Dear Lord,

Whatever it takes, please prepare me for revival. I realize that this could mean being taken out of the comfort zone in a number areas of my life. But that's okay. I want to be on the cutting edge of what You're doing, and how You're doing it.

I submit to the Holy Spirit's dealings in order to be prepared for the worldwide revival and spiritual awakening that is coming. Don't pass me by.

Thank You that You will fulfill what You have purposed for me. I worship You and adore You, my wonderful friend God.

In Jesus' holy name, Amen.

18

Characteristics of Revival Praying

*A*n understanding of the following characteristics of revival praying will enable us to pray with greater effectiveness.

1. Revival praying starts with our recognizing that it is always initiated by God.

God stirs His people to see the need for revival and to know that there's no substitute for it. He motivates us to pray for revival with the understanding that it is something that we cannot organize. It has to be agonized. The relentless "avalanches" of the Holy Spirit's movements are triggered in God's time and way in response to the united cries of God's people (Zechariah 4:6). The psalmist understood this when he cried out, "...*revive us, and we will call on your name*" (Psalm 80:18b).

2. Revival praying involves praying with focused fervor.

As we keep praying the revival prayers of the Old Testament prophets, we sense this and will avoid all generalities or casualness. "*No one calls on your name or strives to lay hold of you*" (Isaiah 64:7a). "*Gird your sword upon your side, O mighty one; clothe yourself with splendor and majesty. In your majesty ride forth victoriously in behalf of truth, humility and righteousness; let your right hand display awesome deeds*" (Psalm 45:3–4).

3. Revival praying requires praying with deliberate definition in relation to sin.

We need to humble ourselves before God for the sin of idolatry in the Body of Christ and be alert to God's strong reaction.

"Has a nation ever changed its gods? (Yet they are not gods at all.) But my people have exchanged their Glory for worthless idols. Be appalled at this, O heavens, and shudder with great horror, declares the LORD. *"My people have committed two sins: They have forsaken me, the spring of living water, and have dug their own cisterns, broken cisterns that cannot hold water"* (Jeremiah 2:11–13).

An idol is something or someone that takes priority in our life over the Lord Jesus Christ, in either our thinking, time, affection, or loyalty; or it hinders our obedience to God. It involves doing our own thing; *"everyone did as he saw fit,"* (Judges 21:25b).

One of the most subtle idols is the preoccupation with ministry responsibilities at the expense of a delighted, devotional, intimate love relationship with the Lord. Note that in the passage from Jeremiah, God said that His people had forsaken *Him*, not that they had forsaken *serving* Him.

We need to identify with the idolatry in our nation. We need to say to God, as Nehemiah did, substituting the name of our nation for the nation of Israel:

"let your ear be attentive and your eyes open to hear the prayer your servant is praying before you day and night for your servants, the people of Israel. I confess the sins we Israelites, including myself and my father's house, have committed against you. We have acted very wickedly toward you. We have not obeyed the commands, decrees and laws you gave your servant Moses" (Nehemiah 1:6–7).

Each nation evidences a far greater love for worldly pursuits than for the pursuit of God.

Priority is given to such areas as sports, pleasure seeking, food, sex, education, hobbies, lust for power, making money, and having more possessions. We need to ask God to convict us by His Spirit if any of these or other areas of idolatry apply to us personally, and if so, repent before Him. As we repent of our sins, God promises to revive us.

"*And it will be said: 'Build up, build up, prepare the road! Remove the obstacles out of the way of my people.' For this is what the high and lofty One says—he who lives forever, whose name is holy: 'I live in a high and holy place, but also with him who is contrite and lowly in spirit, to revive the spirit of the lowly and to revive the heart of the contrite'* " (Isaiah 57:14–15).

We need to pray with the prophet of old, "LORD, *I have heard of your fame; I stand in awe of your deeds* [What you've done in past revivals], O LORD. *Renew them in our day, in our time make them known...*" (Habakkuk 3:2). In other words, we need to ask God to do it again and more, *this* desperate day and in *our* hour of need.

Because Habakkuk believed that God would answer, he added "*in wrath remember mercy*" (verse 2). We then read, "*God came*" (verse 3), manifesting Himself in holiness, glory, majesty, judgment, and awesome power. The same God will answer our prayer for revival.

4. Praying for revival is desperate praying.

This kind of praying comes from the hearts of people who know there's a desperate need, and become desperate for God to meet that need. These people are not self-conscious. They pray with intensity. In submission and obedience to the Holy Spirit's promptings, such intensity can be manifested by strong weeping, groaning, wrestling, and fasting—any one, or all four. Hannah's life illustrates the fact that desperate praying can also be experienced in total silence (1 Samuel 1:13–16).

When Nehemiah heard of the desperate needs of God's people, he said, "*I sat down and wept. For some days I mourned and fasted and prayed before the God of heaven*" (Nehemiah 1:4b).

An even more vivid illustration of desperate praying is found in the book of Ezra. Ezra has learned about the disobedience of spiritual leaders and of the people in marrying foreign women:

"When I heard this, I tore my tunic and cloak, pulled hair from my head and beard and sat down appalled. Then everyone who trembled at the words of the God of Israel gathered around me because of this unfaithfulness of the exiles. And I sat there appalled until the evening sacrifice. Then, at the evening sacrifice, I rose from my self-abasement, with my tunic and cloak torn, and fell on my knees with my hands spread out to the LORD my God and prayed: 'O my God, I am too ashamed and disgraced to lift up my face to you, my God, because our sins are higher than our heads and our guilt has reached to the heavens'" (Ezra 9:3–6).

You, like I, may have been praying consistently for revival for several decades or more, and not yet seen many of the answers. Be encouraged; no prayer has been wasted. All prayers are safe in God's prayer bank and will be cashed in His perfect time. In the meantime, God will encourage us in some tangible way that what we're praying is right on target. What God starts and energizes, He completes. It's His vision and burden.

Long before the Olympic Games were to be held in Los Angeles in 1984, a large international interdenominational evangelistic outreach had been planned to coincide with the Games. Many thousands would participate, and thousands would respond to the gospel through many forms of outdoor witnessing, mostly one on one.

For many months before the Olympics, God had burdened many to meet regularly to pray for the outreach and to pray for revival.

One day, Pastor Dan Sneed, my son John, and I had met to intercede for the outpouring of the Holy Spirit over the greater Los Angeles area of 13 million people.

The more we prayed, the more God encouraged us to pray by increasing the burden. We neither dictated nor claimed the timing for God's answers. On this particular occasion, I was asking God to hold back the judgment we so deserved and pleading His mercy for our city. I was weeping with intense desire for revival, crying out as though my very life depended on gaining the request from Him. I stopped and said to the

Lord, "You've heard my desperate cry. What do you say?" Immediately God directed me to the book of Hosea. *"As surely as the sun rises, he will appear; he will come to us like the winter rains, like the spring rains that water the earth"* (Hosea 6:3b). I worshiped God and wrote the date and occasion in the margin of my Bible.

In January 1993, our pastor, Dr. Jack Hayford, had called the congregation to a solemn assembly. The primary purpose was to seek God's face unhurriedly, in humility, repentance, and intercession for our city and nation. It was a powerful, refreshing time of waiting on God, expecting Him to speak.

While I was interceding quietly but desperately for revival for our city, I stopped and asked God whether there was something from His Word He wanted to give me that related to my focused praying. Once again He clearly directed me to Hosea 6:3.

About ten minutes later, I overheard two men on the church staff talking quietly. One said, "God has just quickened a promise to me of an outpouring of His Spirit that is coming on our city." It was Hosea 6:3. Hallelujah! God is faithful. I expectantly wait the fulfillment of God's sure promise.

5. Praying for revival means travailing unto birth.

A burden for revival is conceived in our spirits by the Holy Spirit. Our part is to ask for such a burden, submit to the person of the Holy Spirit, obey His promptings, and keep praying for revival.

God causes the burden to increase until it is unthinkable not to pray. We are compelled by the vision, the burden, the expectancy, and the promise that there are no still births (Isaiah 66:7–9). The original spark of desire and commitment to pray, ignited and fanned by the flame of the Holy Spirit will not be quenched (Ezekiel 20:47). We take no rest and give God no rest until He answers, just as He tells us in Isaiah 62:6–7.

We understand and are encouraged by the intercessor's role in Isaiah 21:12: *"The watchman replies, 'Morning is coming, but also the night. If you would ask, then ask; and* come back yet again'" [emphasis added]. We do. Repeatedly.

God is also looking for intercessors who will receive His burden to travail for the new births of multitudes who have heard the gospel but have not yet responded. *"This day is a day of distress and rebuke and disgrace, as when children come to the point of birth and there is no strength to deliver them"* (Isaiah 37:3b).

6.   We need to delight in God's sovereignty.

By that I mean that we need to come to the place where our motives are purified when we pray for spiritual awakening. It means that we don't make suggestions to God as to where He starts geographically. We'd be delighted if it was in the church of a denomination other than our own or among a handful of unknown Christians in Anywheresville. We are unconcerned about whom God uses to work through in revival or how He chooses to manifest Himself. We're not concerned about our reputation, only His; we're willing to be identified with all of God's children. God certainly is.

7.   We must believe God for the deluge.

Without faith, our prayers do not impress God. When we read the promises He has given us from His Word, faith rises in our hearts:

"Ask the LORD for rain in the springtime; it is the LORD who makes the storm clouds. He gives showers of rain to men..." (Zechariah 10:1a).

"For I will pour water on the thirsty land, and streams on the dry ground..." (Isaiah 44:3a).

"For as the soil makes the sprout come up and a garden causes seeds to grow, so the Sovereign LORD will make righteousness and praise spring up before all nations" (Isaiah 61:11).

"As surely as the sun rises, he will appear; he will come to us like the winter rains, like the spring rains that water the earth" (Hosea 6:3b).

"From the west, men will fear the name of the LORD, and from the rising of the sun, they will revere his glory. For he will come like a pent-up flood that the breath of the LORD drives along" (Isaiah 59:19).

"Listen to me, my people; hear me, my nation: The law will go out from me; my justice will become a light to the nations. My righteousness draws near speedily, my salvation is on the way, and my arm will bring justice to the nations. The islands will look to me and wait in hope for my arm" (Isaiah 51:4–5).

"The nations will fear the name of the LORD, *all the kings of the earth will revere your glory. For the* LORD *will rebuild Zion and appear in his glory"* (Psalm 102:15–16).

"For Zion's sake I will not keep silent, for Jerusalem's sake I will not remain quiet, till her righteousness shines out like the dawn, her salvation like a blazing torch" (Isaiah 62:1).

"The LORD *will lay bare his holy arm in the sight of all the nations, and all the ends of the earth will see the salvation of our God"* (Isaiah 52:10).

After revival praying in Joel 1:12–17, we have the following promise: *"Be glad, O people of Zion, rejoice in the* LORD *your God, for he has given you the autumn rains in righteousness. He sends you abundant showers, both autumn and spring rains, as before"* (Joel 2:23).

DO YOU HAVE A VISION AND A BURDEN FOR REVIVAL?

- Are you convinced that it is the will of God to bring a great spiritual awakening in your nation?
- Does your prayer life reflect this conviction?
- If revival for your nation depended on your prayer life, do you believe God would bring it?
- Has revival praying become a passion, and are your prayers desperate?
- Are you familiar with the prayers for revival in the Word of God, and the promises that He will send it? Are they an integral part of your revival praying?
- Do you have a world vision in revival praying? Are you *believing* for an outpouring of God's Spirit in spiritual awakening for *every nation* of the world because you are praying for this?

- Have you waited on God and let Him search your heart over your motives in relation to revival?
- Does it matter *where* God starts to pour out His Spirit? Have you preconceived ideas, preferences, and suggestions?
- Do you have reservations about whom He chooses to work through to bring revival, and whom to use in it?
- Are you concerned about *how* God manifests Himself in revival—remembering that the unpredictable and the unusual are the normal?

This chapter needs to be applied not only to our church, but also to our city, our county, our state, our nation, and every country of the world. *"My house will be called a house of prayer for all nations"* (Mark 11:17b).

SUGGESTED PRAYER

Dear God,

I will give you an honest response to the above questions. Show me Your perspective on the importance of revival praying in my life. I will make any necessary adjustments. Deepen the work of Your Spirit in me as I commit to going deeper in intercession for the end time display of Your blazing glory and manifest presence among the nations.

Thank You that You will answer this sincere request. In Jesus' wonderful name, Amen.

19

Where to Begin and How to Continue

*I*f you're wondering how to start on the adventure of intercession, that's good. You've already taken the first step. You begin with a *desire* to be an effective intercessor. Next, you *determine* to be one. The follow-through is to *discipline* your life so that you become one. Don't be intimidated by your lack of experience. Just as a runner learns to run by running, you learn to pray by praying.

Bring yourself, just as you are, to the Lord Jesus and present your prayer life to Him like the little boy did with his unimpressive lunch. The boy must have believed that Jesus would do something miraculous with it for him to have given it away. His was an act of surrender and availability to Jesus. It was also a remarkable act of faith. The Father then miraculously multiplied those five small barley rolls and two small fish in response to Jesus' acts of obedience and faith, and a hungry multitude, including the little boy, was fed (John 6:9–12).

In the same way, the Holy Spirit will work in us and through us, and will supernaturally multiply our effectiveness in intercession as we keep presenting our yielded, repentant lives to His control and direction.

I can recall the time many years ago when I was first learning to intercede for others when praying alone, without the inspiration of group praying. I prayed for fifteen minutes and was all done. That was hardly impressive, and I knew it. But I said to God, "I'll be back, same time, same place tomorrow." And I was. And I came back repeatedly. The more I gave myself to God in prayer for others, the more the Holy Spirit enabled me to pray with both direction and energy. The growth in my own spiritual life in that six month period was accelerated far beyond anything I had previously experienced. I learned that the more we pray for others, the less we'll need to pray for ourselves.

It was my habit each year for my birthday to ask God to quicken to me a verse of Scripture that, when applied, would be particularly relevant to deepening my spiritual growth. A year or two after I began doing this, God responded to my birthday request through my daily Bible reading. This is how God revealed the verse to me:

"Behold, I [the living, eternal, all powerful God] will [definitely, without any doubt] make [create] you [personally] into a new [something you haven't been before] threshing sledge [in intercession] with sharp [effective] teeth [you'll be equipped]; you shall thresh the mountains and beat them small, and make the hills like chaff [great changes shall come among the nations, and nothing shall be impossible through the power of the Holy Spirit as you pray]" (Isaiah 41:15 NKJV).

The process of separating the kernel of the grain from the husks and chaff is called threshing. Threshing in the preceding Scripture is likened to intercession in two other biblical references. In Isaiah 66:7–9, intercession for a nation is likened to the kind of travail a woman has in labor before a child is born. In Micah 4:9–10, the same analogy is used. The call to arise and thresh is given, linking intercession with threshing. Nation-changing results are assured:

"Rise and thresh, O Daughter of Zion, for I will give you horns of iron; I will give you hoofs of bronze and you will break to pieces many nations. You will devote their ill-gotten gains to the LORD, *their wealth to the* LORD *of all the earth"* (Micah 4:13).

Notice the similarity of wording in these two passages to Isaiah 41:15. While God powerfully used Isaiah 41:15 to encourage me at the time, I firmly believe He had another purpose for making it come so alive, that is, that having acted upon the truth as a way of life, I may strongly urge and encourage other believers to believe the promise and act upon it. Read the verse slowly, meditate on it until you believe it, and be inspired to give yourself to God in prayer on behalf of others—especially nations and people groups.

Becoming an intercessor is not complicated. When young Mary heard the angel's startling announcement that she, a virgin, was going to have a child, her response was flawless: *"May it be to me as you have said"* (Luke 1:38b). It was the epitome of humility and faith. Mary expressed total belief, total acceptance of the consequences, and total trust in God's ability to perform the miraculous. Her reaction came from the simple explanation of how the humanly impossible was going to become possible: "The Holy Spirit will come upon you" (verse 35).

Our response to Isaiah 41:15 should be exactly the same. To the degree we yield to the Holy Spirit, ask and believe for His control, obey His promptings, and believe He's working, we too shall have a prayer life that can be explained only by God. And remember that God cannot do anything mediocre.

OUR MAJOR RESPONSIBILITIES

It is so much easier to discharge our responsibilities in intercession if we know what they are and have a plan to cover them on a regular basis. The following categories can be covered in prayer weekly, taking several each day. They can be taken over two or three weeks or a month. Our circumstances and responsibilities vary greatly according to the seasons of our life. The main thing is to endeavor to cover these responsibilities consistently. Ask God to show you His plan for you, and believe that He will. At one stage of my life I found combining worship, intercession, and brisk walking first thing every morning to be a very therapeutic combination. But God knows what's best for each of us.

We need to intercede for:

1.   **Our immediate family members and other relatives,** especially those who are non-Christians (see chapter 4 for the latter category).

2.   **Our God-given gifts of friendship** (see chapter 3).

3.   **Every nation of the world** (see chapter 8) with emphasis on God's people (see chapter 9).

4.   **Spiritual leaders** (see chapter 10).

5.   **Leaders of authority and influence in the nations of the world** (see chapter 11).

6.   **The lost souls God brings across our path to whom we witness.** Make a list of their names or a brief description of the people and the location of the witness as a reminder. Don't give up interceding. You could be the only one praying for them.

7.   **The unconverted, whenever the gospel is being presented to them and we are present.** This includes when we're listening to the sharing of the gospel on the radio or when we're watching television.

I am convinced that thousands more would be converted if we made it a way of life to discipline ourselves to intercede for the salvation of the lost at these times. I find the exercise to be rewarding and fulfilling, as I believe God answers my prayers, and those of many others who pray likewise .

8.   **The unconverted in our city, town, neighborhood and street.**

A tall, blue-eyed, curly headed young man once approached me and said, "You don't know me, but I have wanted to meet you for a long time." I had returned to New Zealand to visit my dear mother while she was still alive and was staying at the home of my cousins, David and Dale Garratt. The young man, whose name was Jeff, belonged to my cousin's church fellowship and had brought us some fresh fish.

Jeff went on to say that he wanted to thank me from the bottom of his heart for faithfully interceding for his soul to be saved. My expression revealed obvious surprise, especially when I heard that he thought my intercession was the most significant factor in relation to his conversion two years previously. I was not aware of having met him or knowing anything about him.

Jeff then explained that for all of his childhood he had lived at Aldersgate Road, Hillsborough, Auckland, New Zealand. At no time was he exposed to any Christian witness or influence from his parents or other relatives. He became exposed to the gospel as an adult in his twenties, and had committed his life to Christ, being the only member of his family (immediate and extended) who was a Christian. He always marveled that he had discovered the way of salvation alone, and wondered why God had brought the influences and pressures to bear to bring him to Christ.

Then one day he met my son John when he had returned to New Zealand to minister. In the course of conversation, John said he remembered that I had prayed consistently for many years for every lost soul on our street to be converted.

Light bulbs of understanding immediately flashed in Jeff's mind. So *that* was the cause of his search for the truth and his quick response to the gospel.

We had lived at Aldersgate Road, Auckland, New Zealand, for many years before going to America. Jeff was a child for part of that time. His six-foot two-inch frame bent over towards my five-foot one-inch body, as he said, "Could I please hug you while I thank you for those many prayers on my behalf?" It was a tender and precious moment. Fulfillment and encouragement abounded.

It is altogether possible that we are the only one praying for the unconverted in our neighborhood or on our street.

9. **The youth and children in the nations** (see chapter 6).

10. **The nation from which we originated and the nation in which we presently live, if it is a different nation.**

11. **The church fellowship to which God directs us.** Our primary responsibility is to intercede for those in leadership (see chapter 10) and pray that they and their followers will apply the principles in chapters 17 and 18.

12. The missionary organizations or other special interest groups to whom we may be directed by God to be committed. Make application as stated in the previous point.

13. The city in which we live. (The vast majority of people in the world live in cities.) *"But seek the welfare of the city where I have sent you...and pray to the Lord on its behalf, for in its welfare you will find your welfare"* (Jeremiah 29:7 RSV). The principles of praying for the Church in the nations as outlined in chapter 9 are equally applicable to praying for cities.

It is important to pray that God will stir the heart of a spiritual leader or leaders in our cities to initiate the coming together of other spiritual leaders across racial and denominational lines to intercede regularly for an outpouring of God's spirit in our cities. This is happening in increasing numbers of cities throughout the world with powerfully significant results.

14. When we hear about disasters and tragedies. We can make it a way of life to pray as God directs us in these situations. Knowledge brings responsibility. Never minimize the effectiveness of our role in such situations.

My dear former secretary, Kay Matta, returned home one afternoon at 5:00 and turned on the television. A special news report was being shown of a fire in an apartment building in downtown Los Angeles. Several victims were lying on the pavement receiving cardiac pulmonary resuscitation (CPR) from paramedics. Then two firemen carried out an eight-month pregnant woman, laid her on the ground, and similarly treated her.

Kay immediately stretched out her hands toward the television set and prayed fervently for the lives of the mother and baby to be spared. She also took authority over the enemy in the name of the Lord Jesus Christ in relation to them both.

About ten minutes later, it was reported that the mother, and subsequently the baby, had died. Shocked but undaunted, Kay continued to intercede for their lives to be spared.

While watching the late news the next evening, to her intense delight, Kay heard a doctor tell the story of a pregnant woman who had been a victim of a fire in downtown Los Angeles. The woman had been brought to the hospital and presumed dead. This particular doctor, who had been on duty, recalled that in the emergency room, doctors had detected a faint pulse beat in the woman and a faint heartbeat in the baby. After resuscitating the mother, the doctors performed a Caesarian section, and mother and baby were expected to live.

During the doctor's interview, a videotape was played of the woman lying on the pavement receiving CPR from the firemen. It was the same woman for whom Kay had prayed fervently. The doctor ended his story by saying that doctors don't use the word *miracle* very often, but in this case, the survival of both the mother and the baby was nothing other than a miracle. Kay thanked and praised God for this divine intervention in response to earnest prayer.

15. New converts and needy Christians whom God intermittently brings across the pathway of our life. Paul's responsibility in prayer for those in this category is clearly described as he writes to the Galatian Christians: *"My dear children, for whom I am again in the pains of childbirth until Christ is formed in you"* (Galatians 4:19).

16. Special projects and events related to our individual ministries.

17. The poor and needy. The majority of these people are in the underprivileged nations (such as Bangladesh and Somalia), the inner cities of the world, and refugee camps. God's Word is strong about our responsibility to be involved in meeting the needs of the poor and needy.

"If there is a poor man among your brothers in any of the towns of the land that the LORD *your God is giving you, do not be hardhearted or tightfisted toward your poor brother. Rather be openhanded and freely lend him whatever he needs. Give generously to him and do so without a grudging heart; then because of this the* LORD *your God will bless you in all your work and in everything you put your hand to. There will always be poor people in the land. Therefore I command you to be openhanded*

toward your brothers and toward the poor and needy in your land" (Deuteronomy 15:7–8, 10–11).

Because prayer causes God's hand to be moved, we start by interceding for the poor and needy and continue on a regular, systematic basis. In James chapter 2, we are told to give equal honor to the poor. In 1 John 3:17, we are exhorted to prove that the love of God is in us by giving materially to the needy. We may wonder how we can do this. The needs are overwhelming. Just about every mail delivery in America contains requests for help. This is how I cope:

- I choose to be obedient to the biblical commands.
- I pray regularly for the many who are working directly with the needy, and for the needy themselves in the nations.
- I am committed to being obedient to the promptings of the Holy Spirit related to meeting the needs of the needy as God sovereignly brings them across the pathway of my life. This always includes interesting and fulfilling adventures (I could fill several chapters related to them).

18. Communists, Buddhists, Hindus, Muslims, Shintoists, humanists, atheists, agnostics, uncompleted Jews, animists, cultists and nothingists (see chapter 12).

19. Those who speak against us. Whether Christian or non-Christian. *"...pray for those who persecute you"* (Matthew 5:44).

If we're thinking that the responsibilities in prayer are too great, listen to Paul, that indomitable, pioneering, faithful, victorious, prayer warrior in chains, whose words ring out through the centuries: *"Be joyful in hope, patient in affliction, faithful in prayer"* (Romans 12:12).

If all our other faculties were taken from us and all we had left was a sound mind and a beating heart, we could still be mightily used of God to affect the history of the nations through the marvelous ministry of intercession.

20. Engage in spiritual warfare as directed by the Holy Spirit's promptings.

SUGGESTED PRAYER

Thank You, Lord, for every way in which You help me have a more purposeful prayer life. I'm also thankful that You know and understand everything about me and my circumstances. This means that I can trust You to show me when and how to cover these responsibilities in a systematic, manageable way so that I am fulfilled, but not overwhelmed.

I look forward with keen anticipation to the resultant blessings from this helpful discipline. I take encouragement from the promise of Your enabling grace as I do my part. "...I will pour out...a spirit of grace and supplication..." (Zechariah 12:10a).

You're a wonderful Master. I love You dearly and ask this in Your precious name. Amen.

20

The Ultimate Intercessor

*T*he ultimate intercessor is the beautiful, wonderful, precious Lord Jesus, the one who excites me the most, inspires me the most, challenges me the most, and encourages me the most to choose to live like Him.

Jesus' earthly life stands unique in human history as our greatest mentor and role model—not Moses, not Daniel, not Elijah, not Paul, not praying Hyde, not Rees Howell, not David Brainerd. We will more fully understand the validity of that statement once we understand some of the reasons for which Jesus came to earth:

- To show us what the Father is like (Hebrews 1:3).
- To die upon the cross and make atonement for the sins of the world (1 Peter 3:18).
- To destroy the works of Satan (1 John 3:8).
- To show us how to live. *"To this you were called, because Christ suffered for you, leaving you an example, that you should follow in his steps"* (1 Peter 2:21).

The last reason is pivotal. If we're to follow in His steps, we have to carefully examine His earthly life. When we do, we discover the priority Jesus gave to prayer. In fact, Jesus' life was punctuated by prayer. He never needed a crisis to motivate

Him to pray. This is not surprising when we understand what prayer is, and how Jesus functioned as Son of Man.

Prayer is the act of bringing God into every situation and asking Him to change it from something natural into something supernatural so that He can get all the glory. Jesus was always doing that in relation to the Father. That's why He could say, "*I do not accept praise from men*" (John 5:41a).

In His incomprehensible humility, Jesus laid aside His function of deity as Son of God, retaining His nature of deity in order to function as Son of Man. Only then could He show us how to live. He modeled absolute submission to the Father, absolute availability, absolute dependence, and absolute obedience, which are the fruits of His absolute humility (John 5:30; John 5:19).

The Lord Jesus is our ultimate example of a life lived in humility and faith. This was never more vividly demonstrated than by His prayer life, which proved His total dependence upon the Father. He always believed that the Father would come through because Jesus always did the Father's will. The challenging parallel is "*As the Father has sent me, I am sending you*'" (John 20: 21b).

Prayer proves our dependence upon God. All independence is the height of pride, and prayerlessness is a manifestation of unbelief. A life without prayer says, "I don't need God in this situation, and even if I did pray, what difference would it make?"

Many Christians pray only when in trouble. Some pray when others ask them to pray. Relatively few make prayer a priority in their personal life, and these are the ones who are always calling others to pray. They believe Jesus' words: "*...apart from me you can do nothing [spiritual]*" (John 15:5b).

Although this final chapter is slanted toward spiritual leaders, since Jesus is the role model for every believer, we all need to apply the principles He lived by. Jesus the leader so obviously made prayer a priority in His own life that His followers asked Him to teach them on the subject (Luke 11:1). It is significant to note two things here:

1. Jesus' disciples didn't ask Jesus to teach them how to lead or preach or teach or administrate or communicate—although He'd certainly be the expert in all those skills. They must have concluded that somehow His prayer life was the key to His remarkably effective ministry and leadership.

2. The disciples' request didn't come because Jesus was always talking about the benefits of prayer or was always planning prayer events. Their request came as a result of seeing Him so frequently in prayer. Many times, leaders spend more time planning prayer events and discussing prayer strategies than actually praying. Not Jesus! He was real.

If we're spiritual leaders we need to answer the following questions:

- What strengths do people under our leadership associate with our life? Would prayer be one?
- Are the people under our leadership inspired and challenged to have a more effective prayer life (especially for others) as a result of our life?
- Are we like Jesus, the leader? Or do we need to change our priorities?

3. Jesus came for another reason—to be our life. "...*Christ in you, the hope of glory*" (Colossians 1:27b). This means that we can consciously, willfully lean on Him to do in us and through us what we know we cannot do ourselves. We cannot live this life of prayer for others without His divine enabling. He knows this and has provided His all-powerful, all-sustaining life for us to depend on moment by moment. What a relief!

"...*Christ lives in me. The [prayer] life I live in the body, I live by faith in the Son of God, who loved me and gave himself for me*" (Galatians 2:20b). In other words, Jesus is saying, "I am in you to live My life through you so that I become the explanation of an effective (prayer) life from you."

THE PRIORITY OF PRAYER IN JESUS' LIFESTYLE

1. **We find Jesus praying at His baptism just before He begins His public ministry.**

God's response was to open heaven, empower Jesus with the Holy Spirit, and audibly speak His approval of His son (Luke 3:21–22). Jesus modeled:

a. The need to minister to the Father before ministering to the people.

b. That the power of the Holy Spirit is essential for effective service.

c. That such power is given in answer to prayer.

We learn that our public ministry is only as powerful as our prayer life, and that God's approval of us is made public, in time, when we make God's priorities ours.

2. Jesus demonstrated His need for prayer during times of great acceptance by the people of His public ministry.

Jesus' ministry included preaching, teaching, and frequent demonstrations of the miraculous as He met multitudinous human needs. It is significant that all four gospels record incidents of Jesus' praying in such circumstances. Many lives were obviously deeply impacted by His example of right priorities.

Often our greatest times of temptation to fail to pray are during seasons of popularity, and when God's power is being manifest through us the most. Let's look at the disciples' record about Jesus' prayer life.

Luke describes a typical day in the life of the Lord Jesus in chapter 5 of his gospel. The people crowded around Jesus listening to His teaching. The reports of a spectacular healing of a leper caused great multitudes to come and hear Him and be healed of their sicknesses. *"But Jesus often withdrew to lonely places and prayed"* (verse 16). The literal translation is, "He was withdrawing and praying," meaning He did this as a way of life.

Mark's report is enlightening: *"...his fame spread everywhere..."* (Mark 1:28 RSV). After being in the synagogue one day, Jesus healed Peter's mother-in-law. That evening, the whole city turned up at His door, and He healed many who were sick and cast out many demons.

Immediately following this account, we read the secret to Jesus' successful ministry. *"Very early in the morning, while it was still dark, Jesus got up, left the house and went off to a solitary place, where he prayed"* (verse 35). Finally, after looking everywhere for Jesus, His disciples found Him praying. It was only then that Jesus announced His schedule for the day. That new day included extensive travel, preaching in the synagogue, casting out demons, and healing the sick. Jesus didn't excuse Himself from taking time alone with Father God first, on the basis that He would need more sleep so that He could cope with God's schedule for Him. Rather, His strength was renewed because He sought and waited on the Father. Jesus obviously considered it important enough to seek God for His schedule, rather than presume what God had planned for Him to do (even though it meant getting less sleep).

Jesus never acted presumptuously, because He was never proud. Pride sees no need to seek God in detail to make sure we're the right person, at the right time, in the right place, with the right condition of heart including the right motivation. *"The LORD looks down from heaven on the sons of men to see if there are any who understand [act wisely RSV], any who seek God"* (Psalm 14:2).

Have we received divine guidance for our ministry assignments? Do we seek God's face until we've heard His voice before accepting a speaking engagement? Are we ready to seek God and obey Him should He want us to move on to the next ministry assignment when there are obvious signs of His grace and power upon us in our present location?

Matthew describes another typical day in Jesus' life in chapter 14 of his gospel that is loaded with "heavy happenings." Jesus' cousin, John the Baptist, had been murdered. As soon as Jesus heard about it, He went to a remote place to be alone, but the usual huge crowds followed Him. Out of great compassion, He put their needs ahead of His own and healed their sick. After that, He prayed, and then organized the miraculous feeding of five thousand men, plus women and children. Quite a day!

Jesus would need some well-earned relaxation. His heart would be heavy over the loss of His fearless cousin John. How

Jesus loved and admired him. Jesus' mind and body would be weary from ministering to thousands of needy people. His spirit would need refreshing. After dismissing the disciples and the crowd, and before giving Peter an unforgettable lesson before dawn on how to walk on water, Jesus followed His favorite rest and relaxation routine—alone with God in prayer.

What would we have done? What do we do when we're feeling drained from ministry responsibilities? Watch TV (good or bad)? Go out and overeat? Sit up late talking to friends for hours to unwind? Go on a shopping spree? Many spiritual leaders do. Not Jesus. He had a better way.

John's account of the priority Jesus gave to prayer as a way of life challenges me the most. It relates to the timing of Jesus' comprehensive and deep prayer for His present and future disciples, as recorded in chapter 17 of John's gospel.

Could any other intercessory prayer be more historic or its implications more encompassing? Jesus repeatedly asked the Father to bring every child of God to complete unity with every other child of God, even as the three persons of the Trinity are united (verse 11).

The implications of Jesus' prayer stagger our imagination and stretch our faith when we ponder how the Church has been characterized by division down through the centuries. World evangelization is dependent upon and will be the result of God's answers to that prayer. *"May they be brought to complete unity to let the world know that you sent me and have loved them even as you have loved me"* (John 17:23b).

Here's the point I want to make. That prayer was prayed after what must have been many hours of some of the most penetrating, potent teaching that ever came through the Lord Jesus. That teaching includes all of chapters 13, 14, 15, and 16 of John's gospel. The prayer also comes after the trauma of Judas' betrayal and the full knowledge of Peter's forthcoming denial—both intensely emotionally draining.

Wouldn't most of us think that we desperately needed some relaxation; a break from the spiritual intensity; have someone else meet our emotional needs? I know I would. I don't profess to have attained to living all the challenging truths in this chapter. But I'm aspiring to do so, by God's enabling grace.

What did Jesus do? The deeper the teaching and the longer He taught, the deeper He went in prayer and the longer He prayed for those He taught. Intercession never took a secondary place in Jesus' ministry of preaching, teaching, and meeting the needs of people's minds, bodies, souls, and spirits.

3. **When Jesus prayed, revelation of truth came to others.**

Once when Jesus was praying privately and His disciples were with Him, He asked them what the crowds said about His identity. After they gave varied answers, Jesus asked the disciples pointedly who *they* thought He was. Peter answered that Jesus was the Christ, the Son of the living God (see Luke 9:18–20). Jesus blessed Peter and stated that this truth could only have come by revelation from God, His Father (see Matthew 16:17).

I believe there is a direct connection between Jesus' private prayer and Peter's response. As Jesus no doubt interceded for the disciples to receive revelation of truth, the Father answered.

We learn from the Lord Jesus that it's not sufficient for a teacher to have revelation of truth and to teach it. Teachers have a responsibility to intercede for revelation to be given by the Holy Spirit to those they teach. We also learn that because prayer was a way of life for Jesus, He took time to pray privately even when the disciples were near Him.

4. **Jesus took time to pray while He was teaching.**

We now see a fascinating glimpse of the Lord Jesus as He spontaneously breaks into joyous thanksgiving and praise to God right in the middle of a teaching time:

"The seventy-two returned with joy and said, 'Lord, even the demons submit to us in your name.' He replied, 'I saw Satan fall like lightning from heaven. I have given you authority to trample on snakes and scorpions and to overcome all the power of the

enemy; nothing will harm you. However, do not rejoice that the spirits submit to you, but rejoice that your names are written in heaven.' At that time Jesus, full of joy through the Holy Spirit, said, 'I praise you, Father, Lord of heaven and earth, because you have hidden these things from the wise and learned, and revealed them to little children. Yes, Father, for this was your good pleasure' " (Luke 10:17–21).

There was nothing formal or stereotyped about Jesus' prayer life. This instance was an outburst of joyous, unself-conscious worship, giving the glory where it belonged. When we're God-conscious, we're not self-conscious.

Jesus was thrilled at hearing the reports of the seventy-two disciples as they returned from their first successful short-term missions outreach. He was thrilled that they had the simplicity and humility of heart to believe and act upon the truths that their Master had taught them about their authority over demonic spirits as they exercised faith in His name.

5. To get direction on who to have as His closest team members, Jesus spent all night in prayer with the Father (see Luke 6:12–13).

Was it because Father God had withheld all their names until the light of day? Was it because Jesus had heard His Father tell Him some, but not all, of their names before dawn? Was it because God had given Him the names in the first few minutes or first hour and Jesus had spent the rest of the night interceding for the twelve men God had chosen?

We don't know the answers to those questions. What we do know is that regardless of the personal cost to Him, Jesus in His humility sought God on behalf of the men He was going to lead until the Father released Him. What a leader! Jesus presumed nothing. And He never tempted the disciples to presume by asking them to join His team without His first hearing from God.

So much disunity in the Body of Christ comes from the lack of waiting on God for specific direction, especially as it relates to ministry appointments and assignments. This lesson from Jesus' life needs to be heeded equally by the leaders who do the inviting and the people who consider accepting the invitation. *"But as for me, I will look to the Lord, I will wait for the God of my salvation; my God will hear me"* (Micah 7:7 RSV); *"I will instruct you and teach you in the way you should go; I will counsel you and watch over you"* (Psalm 32:8).

I will not quickly forget the nine long years I waited for God to bring me the right secretary. I wanted someone called of God and committed. Someone who would share the vision of getting to the nations of the world the truths that God had revealed to me about His character and His ways. Someone who feared the Lord and had the godly wisdom that accompanies it. Someone gifted and graced with the ministry of helps in a secretarial role.

As the workload increased, compounded by endless international traveling and speaking, people would often say to me, "Why don't you just hire someone?" My response was always the same, "I'm waiting for my Isaac. I don't want an Ishmael" (see Genesis 15:4–5 and 16:1–4).

I could hardly believe it when it happened. I'd waited so long. God spoke clearly to a young woman in YWAM whom I had never met personally who offered to serve me. Her name was Janet Izett (pronounced with a long "I," as in Isaac!).

The characteristics I listed describe Janet to a "T." God readily confirmed to me that she was the person of His choosing, as perfect for me as Isaac was for Abraham. I told Janet so.

Was it hard to wait for God's appointed person when the need was so great? Yes, very. Was Janet worth waiting for? A thousand times, yes. What purposes did God have in keeping me waiting? He was testing me. He wanted to see whether I would take on somebody without having His clear direction. He wanted to see whether I would trust Him

- for enabling grace to get through the heavy workload without a secretary.
- to believe that through the long delay of unanswered prayer He would ultimately bless me with someone who would make the waiting worthwhile.

God did. He brought me an outstanding young woman. Dear Janet not only was with me for two years but also later, after she was married and had two children, returned and helped me part-time for another three years and eight months, right up until seven days before delivering her third child. Talk about commitment!! My gratitude to God and to Janet is deeper than I can adequately express.

At a later time, I waited ten months for God to provide me with secretarial help. They were some of the most difficult months of my life up to that time. God knows. Although my husband did everything he could to help, the workload in every area of my life was greater than I had ever had to carry. I had no understanding why there was no relief. I just clung to my knowledge of the character of God and by His grace trusted Him in the dark.

It happened suddenly. One phone call from Janet resulted in the breakthrough. Her friend, Kay Matta, with a heart for God and for missions, became another incredible provision and wonderful gift directly from "Headquarters Heaven." Kay was called of God, committed, wise, skillful, and absolutely delightful. Her anointed ministry of helps was a vitally important and integral part of getting this book published. And God knows how perfectly suited to me she was through the ensuing three years of much physical suffering since I started writing the book. (For over two years the manuscript lay untouched.) My gratitude to God and Kay is very deep.

Once again I proved the following powerful truth: "...no eye has seen any God besides you, who acts on behalf of those who wait for him" (Isaiah 64:4b).

6. Jesus took His closest trainees on a prayer retreat.

"...Jesus...took Peter, John and James with him and went up onto a mountain to pray. As he was praying, the appearance of his face changed, and his clothes became as bright as a flash of lightning" (Luke 9:28–29).

It is significant that the transfiguration of Jesus did not take place while He was preaching in the synagogue or preaching to the outdoor crowds or teaching His disciples or performing miracles. It occurred while He was praying.

The same was true of Moses, the man who loved being alone with God, and the greatest intercessor recorded in the Old Testament. His face also shone with the glory of God.

The more time we spend with God in prayer for others, the more we receive divine perspective, and the more His beauty and glory are evidenced. *"And we, who with unveiled faces all reflect the Lord's glory, are being transformed into his likeness with ever-increasing glory, which comes from the Lord, who is the Spirit"* (2 Corinthians 3:18).

What about Peter, James, and John? This mountaintop experience was undoubtedly the most awesome of their lives to that date. Apart from the wonder of seeing Jesus in His dazzling beauty, could they ever forget hearing the audible voice of God exhorting them to stop making presumptuous statements and to listen to His Son's voice?

You'd think the drama of seeing Moses and Elijah come back from the dead and converse with Jesus would have left the trio speechless! On the other hand, it's amazing what dumb things we can say when we're overwhelmed or in shock. (I know. I've said them.) My point here is that this spectacular experience took place because the men went with Jesus to a prayer meeting!

It's also significant that the men nearly missed the impact of this epic event by going to sleep. *"Peter and his companions were very sleepy, but when they became fully awake, they saw his glory and the two men standing with him"* (Luke 9:32).

What have we missed by disobeying God's promptings to pray? And what revelation have we missed by not resisting the temptation to sleep, and not asking in faith for the Holy Spirit's quickening when we did obey?

7. Two significant prayers that Jesus prayed publicly.

Jesus offered one prayer in the midst of His teaching as He faced the price of going to the cross in obedience to the will of God. *"Now my heart is troubled, and what shall I say? 'Father, save me from this hour'? No, it was for this very reason I came to this hour. Father, glorify your name!"* (John 12:27–28a). Once again God the Father responded with an audible voice from heaven to His Son's prayer: *"I have glorified it, and will glorify it again"* (John 12:28b).

Jesus wasn't afraid to bear His soul before His audience at the Holy Spirit's prompting. His God-consciousness always overrode His self-consciousness and audience-consciousness, which is evidence of great humility.

Next we see Jesus praying publicly immediately before raising Lazarus from the dead. Jesus thanked God for hearing Him, explaining that He said this publicly only so that the people would believe that God had sent Him to earth (see John 11:41–42).

Sometimes the Holy Spirit prompts us to pray publicly what we often pray privately so that others can more fully understand God's ways.

8.   The more penetrating our probe of the prayer life of the Lord Jesus, the more the flame of our love for Him is ignited.

I pause to worship and adore my magnificent, matchless Master, as with awe and wonder we approach the scene in the garden of Gethsemane. As a leader and friend, and as Son of Man, Jesus revealed His need of the prayer support, comfort, and understanding of those closest to Him by inviting them to join Him in prayer at a time of intense anguish. *"My soul is overwhelmed with sorrow to the point of death. Stay here and keep watch with me"* (Matthew 26:38b). Such an evidence of His humility, vulnerability, and humanity!

"Going a little farther, he fell with his face to the ground and prayed…" (verse 39a). To lead means to go first. Jesus the leader was always "going a little farther." We can never lead anybody into a deeper relationship and experience with God than we have chosen to go ourselves.

Prostrate before God, Jesus faced the intense agonies of spirit, mind, and soul related to being separated from His Father God while becoming sin as mankind's Redeemer. He had lived in cloudless communion with His Father before time began. The agony of separation and subsequent subjection to His judgment is entirely beyond the comprehension of our finite minds.

Again we pause to worship. Like Moses, we feel like removing our shoes. We are truly on holy and awesome ground. Jesus inquired whether there was any other way. If not, then the Father's will was all that mattered.

I have wondered whether the silence from heaven at this point was because the agony of the Father's heart was too intense to articulate. We must never underestimate the suffering of the Father's unfathomable love.

There was no other way.

Facing the excruciating physical agonies of being flogged, carrying a heavy wooden cross, and then dying by crucifixion were secondary concerns. The fact that Jesus repeatedly returned to His friends to receive comfort and prayer support shows how much He needed them. Jesus marveled at the disciples' inability to comprehend the magnitude of what was taking place, let alone their insensitivity to His needs. God the Father understood and sent an angel to strengthen His beloved Son.

My heart has been broken a number of times over the ultimate aloneness and loneliness of my beautiful, beloved Savior during those darkest hours. Jesus gave Peter, James, and John the greatest privilege and opportunity of their lifetime by inviting them to attend the most historic, dramatic, intense, history-making prayer meeting ever to be held on planet earth. This time—to their great detriment—they missed the purposes of the prayer retreat. They chose sleep.

It is a great privilege for any of us to be allowed to participate in a godly person's deepest hour of sorrow and anguish of heart, during which his or her soul is bared before us and God. The magnitude of the privilege of sharing such a time with Jesus would never again be offered to any living beings.

In Luke's account, we read that Jesus finally said to His three closest men friends, "Get up and pray so that you will not fall into temptation." How much temptation would we have been spared had we been more obedient to God's call to prayer? How many privileges of sharing God's heart have we missed by choosing things of less priority than intercession? May God have mercy on us!

9.   Jesus' intercession on the cross for those who were jeering at Him and had crucified Him is the ultimate example of forgiveness.

"Jesus said, 'Father, forgive them, for they do not know what they are doing' " (Luke 23:34a). It is also the greatest example of supreme unselfishness, unending mercy, and unconditional love. In all His agony, Jesus was more concerned with the needs of others than His own. And that concern was expressed in compassionate prayer for others.

That is what the ministry of intercession is all about.

How could Jesus react this way at such a time? It was a way of life with Him to forgive when wronged and to pray for others. Jesus lived praying, He died praying, and He went up into heaven praying.

Will you, dear reader, accept the challenge of the One who came not only to show us how to live, but also to be our life, and in humility make His priorities yours? When you do, you'll embark on one of the most thrilling and fulfilling ministries known to man, modeled by God's precious, adorable Son, the living, triumphant, undefeated champion, and soon coming King. My lover, Jesus Christ.

Countries of the World

Afghanistan
Albania
Algeria
American Samoa
Andorra
Angola
Anguilla
Antigua & Barbuda
Argentina
Armenia
Aruba
Australia
Austria
Azerbaijan
Bahamas
Bahrain
Bangladesh
Barbados
Belarus
Belgium
Belize
Benin
Bermuda
Bhutan
Bolivia
Bosnia &
   Herzegovina
Botswana
Brazil
British Indian
   Ocean Territory
British Virgin
   Islands
Brunei
Bulgaria
Burkina Faso
Burundi
Cambodia
Cameroon

Canada
Cape Verde Islands
Cayman Islands
Central African
   Republic
Chad
Channel Islands
Chile
China
Christmas Island
Cocos Island
Colombia
Comoros
Congo
Cook Islands
Costa Rica
Cote d'Ivoire
Croatia
Cuba
Cyprus
Czech Republic
Denmark
Djibouti
Dominica
Dominican
   Republic
Ecuador
Egypt
El Salvador
Equatorial Guinea
Eritrea
Estonia
Ethiopia
Faeroe Islands
Falkland Islands
Fiji
Finland
France
French Guiana

French Polynesia
Gabon
Gambia
Georgia
Germany
Ghana
Gibraltar
Greece
Greenland
Grenada
Guadeloupe
Guam
Guatemala
Guinea
Guinea-Bissau
Guyana
Haiti
Honduras
Hong Kong
Hungary
Iceland
India
Indonesia
Iran
Iraq
Ireland
Isle of Man
Israel
Italy
Jamaica
Japan
Jordan
Kazakhstan
Kenya
Kiribati
North Korea
South Korea
Kuwait
Kyrgyzstan

Laos
Latvia
Lebanon
Lesotho
Liberia
Libya
Liechtenstein
Lithuania
Luxembourg
Macao
Macedonia
Madagascar
Malawi
Malaysia
Maldives
Mali
Malta
Marshall Islands
Martinique
Mauritania
Mauritius
Mayotte
Mexico
Micronesia,
   Federated States
Midway Islands
Moldova
Monaco
Mongolia
Montserrat
Morocco
Mozambique
Myanmar
Namibia
Nauru
Nepal
Netherlands
Netherlands Antilles
New Caledonia
New Zealand
Nicaragua
Niger
Nigeria
Niue Island

Norfolk Island
Northern Cyprus
Northern Marianas
   Islands
Norway
Oman
Pakistan
Palau
Panama
Papua New Guinea
Paraguay
Peru
Philippines
Pitcairn Island
Poland
Portugal
Puerto Rico
Qatar
Reunion
Romania
Russia
Rwanda
San Marino
Sao Tome &
   Principe
Saudi Arabia
Senegal
Seychelles
Sierra Leone
Singapore
Slovakia
Slovenia
Solomon Islands
Somalia
South Africa
Spain
Sri Lanka
St. Helena
St. Kitts & Nevis
St. Lucia
St. Pierre &
   Miquelon
St. Vincent
Sudan

Suriname
Svalbard & Jan
   Mayen Islands
Swaziland
Sweden
Switzerland
Taiwan
Tajikstan
Tanzania
Thailand
Togo
Tokelau Islands
Tonga
Trinidad & Tobago
Tunisia
Turkey
Turkmenistan
Turks & Caicos
   Islands
Tuvalu
Uganda
Ukraine
United Arab
   Emirates
United Kingdom
United States of
   America
United States Virgin
   Islands
Uruguay
Uzbekistan
Vanuatu
Vatican
Venezuela
Vietnam
Wallis & Futuna
   Islands
Western Samoa
Yemen
Yugoslavia
Zaire
Zambia
Zimbabwe

Other titles by Joy Dawson...

Some of the Ways of God in Healing

Joy is ruthless in her pursuit of truth on the subject of healing. Truth itself heals. All-out integrity in the probing of Scripture on the subject.

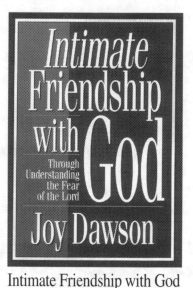

Intimate Friendship with God

This book powerfully motivates the reader to fulfill the biblical conditions for intimate friendship with "the most exciting Being in the universe...Lover-God."

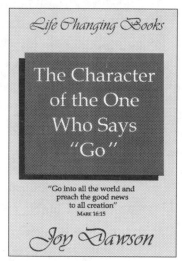

The Character of the One Who Says "Go"

In this booklet, Joy deals with focused intercession and the character of God. This is foundational material for every Christian.

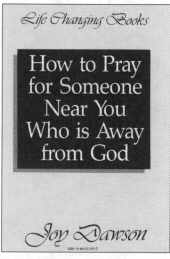

How to Pray for Someone Near You Who is Away from God

A Challenge to believe God and let Him use you as one to effectively "stand in the gap" for those near you.